T0129458

LEADERSHIP
71 IDEAS

REAL LEADERSHIP IS ABOUT
POSITIVE TRANSFORMATION

PAMELA LOYD, PH.D.

authorHOUSE®

AuthorHouse™
1663 Liberty Drive
Bloomington, IN 47403
www.authorhouse.com
Phone: 1 (800) 839-8640

Published by AuthorHouse 10/30/2018

ISBN: 978-1-5462-6648-8 (sc)
ISBN: 978-1-5462-6649-5 (hc)
ISBN: 978-1-5462-6658-7 (e)

Library of Congress Control Number: 2018913015

Print information available on the last page.

Any people depicted in stock imagery provided by Getty Images are models, and such images are being used for illustrative purposes only. Certain stock imagery © Getty Images.

This book is printed on acid-free paper.

Because of the dynamic nature of the Internet, any web addresses or links contained in this book may have changed since publication and may no longer be valid. The views expressed in this work are solely those of the author and do not necessarily reflect the views of the publisher, and the publisher hereby disclaims any responsibility for them.

This publication is intended for the purpose of sharing ideas from the author on the subject matter covered. It is not intended for purposes that may require professional attention and advice. As such, it is not intended as a substitute for any treatment or professional advice you may have received. If you believe you require professional or expert advice, you are urged to seek professional assistance.

Scripture taken from The Holy Bible, King James Version. Public Domain

DEDICATION

If you want to learn some ideas and gain insight about leadership, this book is dedicated to you. It should be noted, the ideas are randomly arranged (i.e., in no particular order) on purpose. You, the reader, are encouraged to think about the ideas and make your own assessment as to which ideas are, perhaps, most useful for you to consider adopting.

CONTENTS

INTRODUCTION

It is interesting to note that it is not unusual for a person to *want* to be a leader. If you watch children playing together, you can see leadership traits emerging. The same is true for adults. When a gathering of adults takes place (e.g., in the workplace), it is likely a leadership attribute of some kind will be evident. Leadership occurs in the home, in the workplace and in other areas (e.g., in churches). Ideally, the goal is to have the right kind of leadership (i.e., effective leadership).

IDEA #1: THE BEST LEADERS KNOW WHEN TO FOLLOW OTHER'S ADVICE

Do you know when to follow someone else's advice? Leadership requires being able to know when it is time to follow the advice of someone else. A leader knows the value of gaining insight from others who have specific knowledge and expertise. When you take into consideration the vast amount of information that is available, it is incumbent upon a leader to be willing to listen to others. This implies being humble.

Leadership is dynamic when it involves the contributions of others. No one person has all the answers. Each person brings unique ideas, thoughts and suggestions. Leaders should embrace advice from others. Ideally, the advice should come from those skilled in the particular area. For example, if a decision has to be made about talent acquisition, a professional in the area of Human Resources Management (HRM) may be consulted.

Taking advice from others is key to effective leadership. Using others' suggestions as a means towards decision-making helps to ensure the best decision is made. This does not mean that a leader will use all of the suggestions offered. Rather, it means the leader will consider the suggestions and determine the usefulness thereof. So, effort has to be made to reach out to others for their expertise. Although this makes perfect sense, it is not always easy to do for some leaders. Inherently, and perhaps all too often, those in leadership positions believe they have all of the insight due to their position or title. They fail to realize the importance of championing the advice of others.

Therefore, key to leadership is the willingness to seek guidance from those who have more experience in particular areas. When a leader desires such expertise, the ability to make in-formed decisions is apparent. Leadership, then, requires aspects of being a follower, too. Put another way, effective leaders know when to follow.

IDEA #2: ETHICS, ETHICS, AND MORE ETHICS

Ethical behavior should be exhibited and encouraged. Leaders are constantly being observed. They should, therefore, display ethics in decision-making and leadership. Ethical behavior reflects doing what is right. Even if doing what is right is difficult or challenging, the best leaders still do it. There is an air about them where they purpose in their heart to stay true to being ethical. The view of ethics is not arbitrary; rather, it is logically derived. It is meaningful from the standpoint of sincerely desiring to make the right choices and decisions.

Ethics seen in a leader instills, motivates and promotes ethics throughout the organization. As such, leadership based on ethics tends to dramatically affect the organization's culture. It is as if ethical behavior becomes a customary practice. It is a norm of the organization. The benefits can be significant.

When the entire organization embraces and acts in an ethical manner, everyone benefits in some way. Those in leadership positions are trusted by subordinates, for instance. Also, leaders trust their employees and may be willing to reward their consistent ethical behavior by empowering them to make certain decisions. Clients or customers are more likely to be properly assisted. Subsequently, they tend to be driven towards being long-term clients or repeat customers. This produces a positive impact on retention strategies. Maintaining customers or clients is an important consideration from a leadership perspective.

Continuously applied ethics demonstrates a leader's dedication to long-term professional relationships. Ethics is necessary and should be observable. The more ethical the leadership, the more ethical the organization is likely to be.

IDEA #3: TIME MANAGEMENT SKILLS

Leadership necessitates time management skills. Meetings (scheduled and unscheduled) can be one the most frequented activities that drain the time available in a workday. The time spent in meetings can vary the same way the type of meetings varies. Leaders have to decide how much time can be allotted to meetings and other activities as well as ensure the availability of time for specific work-related tasks, duties and responsibilities. The essence of effective time management skills, then, is to be able to prioritize.

Leaders must be able to assess the importance of required undertakings. Consequently, they need to eliminate time inhibitors. Prioritization, in its simplest form, means the listing of events to be accomplished from most important to least important. The listing should include indications of estimated time required per task. A checkmark can be used as each activity is completed. Marks such as these can serve as feel-good stimuli reflecting the accomplishment of essential tasks.

Prioritization should be combined with the ability to organize in an effort to enhance time management skills. Interestingly, prioritization tends to come relatively easy for some leaders. But, some do not do so well when it comes to being organized. For some leaders, getting and staying organized can be a daunting undertaking. The key to getting organized is to just start. Begin by organizing important documents, for instance. Next, stay organized. Do not allow yourself to go back to being unorganized by failing to put items back into the appropriate places. Overtime, being organized can become routine making it easy to maintain organization. With prioritization and organization skills mastered, goals or objectives are likely being met.

Meeting goals and objectives is essential for effective leadership. To do otherwise would be counterintuitive to what it means to be a leader. Additionally, being able to prioritize and organize can alleviate unnecessary stress. Unquestionably, time management skills are a virtual impetus to efficient leadership.

IDEA #4: HIGH STANDARDS OF EXCELLENCE

Arguably, there are different perspectives on what constitutes high standards of excellence. Herein, the viewpoint is one of extraordinary expectations. That is, simply put, the best. Effectual leadership must be mindful of the value of superior results. Certainly, leaders should not want mediocrity or below average results. Even average result levels, when overwhelmingly the case, can render negative consequences (esp., long-term). Rather, they should insist upon high standards of excellence in themselves. In addition, leaders should share expectations of high standards of excellence from others.

Therefore, ideally, high standards should be the basis for leadership. In this way, leaders should uphold extraordinary expectations. All outcomes may not meet the standard at all times. Yet, it does not negate the importance of striving for high standards of excellence.

One way to consider inspiring high standards of excellence is to regularly promote it throughout the organization. Everyone needs to be on-board; and, the leader is responsible for accomplishing this goal. Therefore, constant reminders to strive for high standards of excellence are crucial. In other words, it must become a vital part of the organization's idea of itself. From essential job duties to nonessential tasks, high standards of excellence must be fundamental to the organization's existence. Only then will it likely be achieved on a consistent basis.

To be clear, the key is for everyone in the organization, beginning with leadership, to embrace and strive to attain high standards of excellence as a normal part of organizational activities. The right leader will, ideally, be a model expression of high standards of excellence.

IDEA #5: BEST PRACTICES

A common theme (i.e., terminology) used is "Best practices" which suggests researching what works best. It is a worthwhile practice for staying up-to-date and being well-informed in a particular area or industry. Accordingly, leadership needs to do both: stay up-to-date and be well-informed. Frankly, this is not an option if a leader wants to be successful in a myriad of ways.

Best practices should be discovered as well as used where applicable and if feasible. Determining which best practices to incorporate generally is based on similarity of entities (organizations), ease of incorporation and any related cost factors. The potential benefits must outweigh any inherent costs. Leaders have to ascertain which best practices should be utilized and when. Although this is not always an easy determination, it is one that can be remarkable towards reaching organizational improvement, better productivity and increased profitability.

Areas where leadership may be interested in researching best practices vary, esp. based on industry. However, some general guidelines may include areas related to: Human Resources, Technology, Operations Management, Marketing, Organizational Behavior, Quantitative Analysis, Finance and Accounting. Undoubtedly, ethics and customer service are two areas, in particular, where researching and incorporating best practices makes perfect sense. Interestingly, these are two areas where too many leaders fall short. Yet, failing at one or the other, or worse case both, can be detrimental to the leader and the organization. Unfavorable results would definitely be likely.

To be sure, use of best practices, as much as possible, can have positive effects on the organization. Leadership should determine which areas should be researched for best practices. Doing so, perhaps annually, can help the organization stay up-to-date and keep the leader and staff well-informed.

IDEA #6: WE WIN, YOU WIN, I WIN

Leadership is garnered by a fundamental understanding best expressed as "it is not all about me". To some, this may be a common-sense awareness. However, it is not always embraced by some in leadership positions. Leaders who truly comprehend leadership concepts know how vitally important it is to lead others in a way which demonstrates caring about them. Perhaps, this is the real hallmark of leadership. It is reflected in making decisions and choices that are for the betterment of all stakeholders. There is no picking and choosing who to make the best decisions for, in the sense of favoritism, for instance. Leadership at its finest is evidenced when the leader is able to internalize: We win, you win, I win.

Think about it, everyone can benefit in some way based on the direction of leadership. But, the degree of such benefits is likely to vary from time to time. Leaders are keenly aware of this and recognize the value of ensuring fairness as much as possible. To this end, taking an approach where the perspectives of all stakeholders are considered helps leaders to be more impactful overall. Also, frequent displays of using this approach are a masterful way of conveying to others that they are valued. Most, if not all, people want to be viewed as an asset to an organization and leadership.

Winning, then, is conceptualized in leadership when it is based on the vantage point of all of the leaders' stakeholders. It does not imply the idea that everyone should get some type of physical reward, which is the same for all regardless of effort, etc. Quite the contrary, "we win, you win, I win" suggests everyone benefits in some way to some degree. Leadership should clearly convey this message to thwart any attempts by some to infer the leader is unfair. That is, all stakeholders need to know how they benefit from the leader's decision. Hence, the advantage of adopting the "we win, you win, I win" concept is apparent.

IDEA #7: CONSIDER PRAYING BEFORE MAKING DECISIONS AND CHOICES

Making the choice to pray is an individual choice. While it is each individual leaders' choice whether to pray or not, it should at least be considered.

Some leaders may not believe in God. Other leaders may doubt God's existence. Then, there are leaders who are saved/born-again (see St. John 3:3, 5). The Bible is clear; there is only one God who is revealed in three persons: Father, Son (Jesus Christ aka the Word) and Holy Spirt (see 1 John 5:7; 1 John 1:1-3 and St. John 1:1-3). If a leader falls into one of the first two categories, he or she should consider the following: Everyone is a sinner in need of a Savior. Jesus Christ is the *only* Savior. He was *mocked, beaten, shed his blood,* and *died on the cross* for *all* sinners (see Matthew 26:57-27:50). And, *He rose again*! (See Luke 24:1-53). He did this so human-beings who believe in Him could avoid Hell and spend eternity with the Lord (see St. John 3:15-18). Thus, it makes sense to pray to God asking for forgiveness of one's sins, being repentant, and accepting Jesus Christ as Lord and Savior. Everyone (including leaders) should want God's agape love. Suggestion: Read the Bible.

A leader should want to know the truth about God. In a pure sense, leadership is about making the right decisions and choices. To know the truth of the existence of the creator, God (Yahweh), is to know who He is explicitly. Acceptance of God puts leaders in a position of inquiring to (i.e., praying to) God (Adoni) prior to making decisions. God is the ultimate, definitive, *perfect* leader. Any person in a leadership position who desires to make the *right* choices would do well to seek guidance from the perfect leader. Prayer is a way to acknowledge God and need for His counsel. Leaders should resolutely endeavor to do what is right. But, in the long-term (from an eternal perspective), leaders who make the right decisions and choices, based on following God's direction, are the ones who will likely be highly rewarded by God. In the end, rewards from the Lord are the ones that really matter. Perhaps *praying before making decisions and choices*, and doing God's will based on what He tells the leader to do in response to prayer, can lead to rewards from God that are immeasurable.

God's Word—the Bible—is powerful. Sincere prayer to the one and only true living God is also powerful. Moreover, God's response is always right! Leaders should want to make decisions and choices that are right.

IDEA #8: OPPOSING VIEWPOINTS

Leadership requires a willingness to listen to opposing viewpoints. A lot can be gained from doing so. Differing perspectives can be considered. Ideas might emerge pursuant to better decisions. A level of respect can be garnered from those with different views.

It takes a lot, perhaps, for some in leadership positions to consider perspectives different from their own. Nonetheless, this is a necessary component of effective leadership. Reflecting on multiple perspectives allows the leader to have a more holistic or big picture approach to decision-making. No one human-being has all the answers. Leaders need to find value in perspectives that warrant consideration of thought. While the perspectives may or may not have an ultimate effect on the leader's decision, at least the consideration of the perspectives will likely lead to formulation of better choices.

Interestingly, leaders are more likely to make better choices when they are cognizant of ideas presented by others. Take a moment to ponder the vast external differences, as well as internal similarities, which exist between people, in general. It is wonderful when one is able to acknowledge the wonder of how the features of human-beings are different yet similar. In turn, then, leaders should gain an awareness of the value of differing or dissenting viewpoints. The leader has to decide if there is value in incorporating the viewpoints of others for specific situations.

Clearly, the ideas proposed by others can spark additional thoughts for consideration on the part of the leader. Opposing viewpoints allow the thought process to be more complete. That is, acknowledging the value of at least considering thoughts that differ allows a leader to be more insightful in terms of possibilities. Opposing viewpoints can be either useful or not useful. Moreover, including opposing viewpoints in the leader's decision may make sense to do so. Or, conversely, the opposing viewpoints may be unnecessary, ineffectual or of no consequence in the leader's ultimate decision.

Nonetheless, effective leadership acknowledges the importance, and value, of considering opposing viewpoints. It is an aspect of the decision-making process that is not necessarily comfortable or desirable. But, it is needed to have a more comprehensive perspective of ideas and situations towards making the best decisions.

IDEA #9: MORALS, VALUES AND PRINCIPLES

It is not uncommon to hear someone in the workplace environment mention "morals, values and principles". In academia, too, this terminology is expressed. Even in personal or familial settings, at some time or another, someone will likely bring up a topic and include one, two, or all three in some context. Suffice it to say, there is a societal view of the importance of morals, values and principles.

True, and effective, leaders emphasize consistent application of these elements. The leader will ensure practices that communicate to all stakeholders that morals, values and principles are evident throughout the organization. Normal practice, then, will comprise activities that promote constant reflection of the three ideals.

One way to think of morals, values and principles is to use the concept of "righteousness". The leader of the organization must embrace and reflect righteousness in order to perpetuate a work environment where the elements thrive. Embracing righteousness requires a deliberate approach. Therefore, a leader, in the truest sense, will showcase the significance of righteousness by acknowledging it when it is seen in the workplace. This will encourage others to demonstrate they embrace righteousness.

When a leader reflects righteousness, there is awareness by others that the leader makes every effort to do what is right. It is as if a brilliant light is shining directly on the leader. The illumination from a leader who consistently does what is right is fascinating. Interestingly, it is this type of leader who motivates others to do what is right, too. Remarkably, when this is consistently the case, the leader will likely do what is beneficial to all stakeholders in some way and at some level. A righteousness leader does not imply perfection. But, it does assert a desire and willingness to seek perfection and get as close as possible. Demonstrating, and encouraging an environment reflective of, morals, values and principles *just makes sense.*

IDEA #10: INSPIRES

A key attribute of a real leader is one who inspires others. True leaders are not selfish. They want others to be successful. Therefore, this kind of leader will inspire others to excel. Ideally, the leader's inspiration will lead others to significant levels of accomplishment. To put it another way, a leader is one who wants others to do extremely well. As such, it is rather easy to distinguish a leader of this caliber. She or he will purposely influence others to be their best.

Being equipped to be able to encourage others towards excellence, esp. on a regular basis, is extraordinary. This is based on the notion and realization that most people are only interested in what benefits themselves. Effective leadership understands the unseen reward of helping others fulfill their destiny. Inspiring others to be, and do, their best is an act of leadership in that it requires having another person's best interest in mind. This is an essential part of leadership: Leaders are interested in the well-being of others. They want the best for others.

Perhaps this explains why, in reality, there are few real and true leaders. Yet, there are many in leadership positions. Generally speaking, just about any person can occupy a leadership position. Some people are in leadership positions because of *who* they know. Others are in leadership positions because of *what* they know. However, it takes a real leader to do what is best for others. There is no compromise. True leaders say and do what will inspire others towards their best.

Inspiring others is not something done on a whim. It is a purposeful act based on a characteristic of leadership that clearly promotes the ideal that excellence is achievable. Furthermore, when leaders inspire others they press upon them to go beyond mediocrity and envision the possibility of reaching new heights.

IDEA #11: TRANSFORMS

To transform another person so that he or she can take on a new role or additional responsibility is the mark of a leader. Arguably, a person has to want to change (be transformed). When a leader observes this in a person, based on profound insight, the leader will take steps to ensure transformation is reached. In some cases, professional development and training may be required. Other situations may show a need for mentoring.

Having an interest in making others better is clear evidence of a leadership characteristic. It takes a remarkable person to want others to improve and be their best. Furthermore, to actually take action towards the betterment of others is a distinguishing trait of a leader. True leadership requires interest in others.

When an employee, for example, demonstrates a willingness to take on new projects or learn new tasks, this can be a sign of the person's desire to make positive changes. An astute leader will observe this behavior and take on the challenge of ensuring transformation of the employee. That is, the leader will take specific steps towards the realization of the person being transformed. One way to do this, for instance, may be to refer the employee to professional development opportunities. Professional development is an excellent way to transform employees. They can attend various webinars, seminars, online sessions and in-seat classroom sessions geared at introducing new skills or improving existing skills. Professional development, then, becomes a way to improve the employee in a current position or prepare the employee for promotional opportunities. Either way, professional development can be a tool for employee transformation.

In some cases, however, specific training may be needed (which also can be accomplished in varying formats). For example, the employee may require training in an area specific to his or her current position to be more confident in meeting career-specific goals and objectives.

Trainings are typically offered, in some form, at most organizations. The trainings can be interactive, informal or formal. With appropriate training, employees can be transformed by being competent and highly productive.

Mentorship is another avenue worth consideration as a leader endeavors to transform others. The leader can be the mentor or the leader can assign another capable and accomplished person in the organization to be a mentor. Generally, due to leadership's time constraints, the latter may be the preferred approach. An employee tends to transform when consistently gaining insight from someone who has already reached the goal the employee is seeking to acquire. A key reason for the value of mentoring is that there is likely to be a high level of respect for the mentor by the employee receiving the mentorship.

All three, professional development, training and mentoring are effective ways to transform a person towards improvement. Leadership makes it a point to seek out those who display a desire to be better. Then, appropriate action is taken to ensure the explicit result of transformation is achieved. Transformation renews the person. They are more knowledgeable and equipped to accomplish more challenging tasks. The level of awareness of happenings related to the organization, for instance, tends to be more pronounced. Transformation yields marked improvements that are discernable.

IDEA #12: VISIONARY

A visionary has the ability to look ahead (have a futuristic outlook). Although no one knows the future, leadership instinctively warrants the necessity to pursue the future with optimism while being realistic. An essential component of expressing a vision is demonstrating its plausibility. A vision has to be believable to be achievable.

Leaders are capable of "seeing" the future from the perspective of comprehension of current events, knowledge of the past (history) and insight. Leadership needs to be optimistic and realistic. Optimism comes from the leader's insight. Realism is reflective of today and the past. The expressed vision has a way of taking into consideration, therefore, the past the present and the future. This allows the vision to more likely be realized since all time points are included and contemplated.

Leaders need to convey the credibility and reasonableness of the vision. A vision can comprise something not yet experienced or not evident in any way. However, it must be explainable in such a way that its possibility is apparent. One idea for demonstrating the vision's likelihood is to provide examples, simulations, models, graphs, charts or any other visual representative of the vision.

If the vision is not believable, it may be difficult to get buy-in from others. Even if the vision is quite forward-thinking such that no one can completely comprehend it, the leader should showcase scenarios or illustrations so that others are able to envision its possibility and get on-board towards it becoming reality.

Leaders with a vision are leaders with a purpose. This is undeniable. Consequently, visionary leaders can accomplish incredible tasks for the betterment of society.

IDEA #13: UNAFRAID OF FAILURE

Real leaders are not afraid of failing. They recognize this is part of the learning process. Making a mistake or failing helps leaders recognize what does not work or what is ineffective. In some cases, it shows where adjustments are needed. Failure can be considered, from one with a positive outlook, as a closer step towards getting it right or making something better (success). This leadership trait is not apparent in many (arguably, most people). Hence, it helps explain why there are *few* true leaders (yet, unfortunately, many in leadership positions).

Failure is a part of life. Failure is not the problem. It just occurs sometime. The key is the attitude about the failure and what steps are taken following the failure. Leadership insists on an attitude of sincere humility coupled with enthusiasm when failure happens. Failing has a unique way of humbling a person. It encourages the person to contemplate other options and alternatives perhaps not previously considered. Humbling moments are essential for continued growth and maturity as a leader. In essence, the failure (or so-called failure) is really an opportunity to do even more extraordinary things.

Failure is one of the most intense as well as interesting aspects of leadership. Being unafraid of failure is characteristic of real leadership. The light of hope, faith and belief emerges, seemingly instantaneously, when leaders do not allow fear of failure to consume them. Creative thinking and innovation are promising. Constructive ideas become apparent. The brain and heart appear to operate simultaneously at higher levels toward enhanced cognition and better care and concern for how actions affect others, respectively.

Leaders should use failures as opportunities for better outcomes. Amazing outcomes can materialize when experiences of failure have been replaced with humility and enthusiasm.

IDEA #14: EFFECTIVE COMMUNICATOR

An essential expectation of a leader is the ability to communicate effectively. Written, verbal and even non-verbal communications need to be clearly expressed. Articulating thoughts and directives requires communication skills. Leadership needs to convey ideas to others in a linear format. Direct communication tends to result in successful completion of objectives. Leaders who value time and resources understand the need for effective communication.

Written communication in terms of proper use of language skills, esp. in today's technology-driven era, appears to be diminishing. Suffice it to say, maybe it is becoming extinct (or of little importance). Ideally, written communication has a purpose. Leaders are not always able to express themselves verbally. So, there are occasions where written communication is necessary. Impeccable written communication skills help to make sure leadership's desires are understood. The leader may employ someone else to compose and disseminate written communication on the leader's behalf (after the leader has reviewed the contents for accuracy, for example). Nonetheless, the leader will ensure written communication is clearly conveyed.

Verbal communication is perhaps the most frequently used kind of communication. It is certainly great when there is not enough time to communicate in writing (e.g., when the writing would be lengthy). Communicating verbally tends to work well, and is preferable, for some people. Time constraints may prohibit being able to sit down and read a lengthy document. In some cases, frankly, it is better to communicate verbally to be able to address any concerns or answer questions immediately.

Leaders, interestingly, have occasions where they communicate non-verbally. Perhaps written or verbal communication is not warranted or needed; yet, the leader is compelled to communicate to one or more people in some way due to the situation at hand. Thus, non-verbal communication needs to be expressed clearly, too. Clear non-verbal signals from the leader can make a huge difference in how certain situations are handled.

Leaders need to know how and when to communicate. Moreover, they need to know what type of communication technique to use. Clear communication is a leader's "tool" for ensuring goals and objectives are achieved.

IDEA #15: RECOGNIZES THE VALUE OF COLLABORATION

Working with others is beneficial to all aspects of life, including professional. Leadership involves being able to work with others. The leader will invariably need to reach a consensus on many matters. Collaboration encourages leadership to cooperate with various people. Collaboration is an effort where professional relationships can be harnessed to a common goal. Actual goal attainment is the desired result. In order to facilitate collaboration mutual respect is crucial.

Ultimately, the leader makes decisions. However, those decisions are typically made after working with others on the issue. In some cases, the leader does not have to directly be involved in the collaborative efforts. Yet, he or she will be certain to create an atmosphere where collaboration is encouraged, expected and apparent.

Organizations, more often than not, will have to reach a consensus on certain action items. This is especially the case when multiple units or departments will be impacted by the decision. Reaching an agreement can more likely be attained when collaboration is the mechanism utilized. The entities tend to understand the value of, and be focused on, cooperation with one another. Mutual respect for one another will be visible. When people have a cooperating mindset, they tend to be more relaxed, think clearer, and endeavor to accomplish the task at hand. Leadership benefits greatly from this type of collaboration in that it is easier to make any final determinations.

IDEA #16: MISSION-ORIENTED

Effective leadership requires comprehension of the mission. The mission provides a clear direction of desired expectations. Although in many cases the leader determines the mission, there are certain situations where the mission is given to a person in a leadership role. For example, the Board of Directors of an organization may give a directive (mission) to the CEO or President. Carrying out the mission to achieve the desired outcome is an essential component of leadership. Knowledge of the mission is essential for the leader. However, carrying out the mission and achieving the goal or objective requires exceptional leadership skills. Effective leadership, then, is mission-oriented: know the mission; carry it out; and, achieve the desired outcome.

Being mission-oriented begins with determining what is needed to be achieved. That is, what does the leader need to accomplish. Inclusive in the assessment is answering questions, such as: Why does it need to be accomplished? What tools and persons are necessary? Are there any location concerns? Where does the mission need to take place? When is the deadline for mission accomplishment? What costs are involved? Is the mission feasible? Are there other options or alternatives worth considering? How can the achievement of the mission benefit the organization or company (and the stakeholders)? In a nutshell, mission-oriented leaders are cognizant of the importance of being aware.

Probably the hardest part of being a mission-oriented leader is actually carrying out the mission. This step takes all of the necessary resources and utilizes them in the most practical way possible. During the process, it is likely some type of change or reconsideration is needed. Therefore, the leader should be adaptable to necessary changes in the process; yet, remain committed to achieving the mission. A meaningful aspect of carrying out the mission rests with the leader's attitude about the mission. The establishment of effective leadership means that the leader is an independent thinker as well as a team player. Effective leaders, engaged in reaching a goal or objective, will work tirelessly for the team while ensuring his or her own independence in thinking. Both are important in the quest for carrying out the mission. Effective leaders are true to themselves, others and the mission.

Life is full of people who know what they want to achieve. Some people even go so far as to take some of the steps necessary towards reaching their goal. But, only a few actually realize their goal. Exceptional people tend to fulfill their aspirations. Exceptional leaders, consequently, are determined and ultimately accomplish the organization's mission. It is not an option. Rather, it is a must (unless, the mission has been dismissed due to better considerations). As a factor of effective leadership, being mission-oriented is a major character trait.

IDEA #17: KNOW HOW TO MANAGE

Leadership and management are often separated ideals. There are actions expected of leaders and different actions expected of managers. However, there are situations and occasions when leaders need to know how to manage and where managers need to know how to lead. When a leader knows how to manage it is easily discernible. Resources will be managed ensuring accountability. People will be principally managed such that objectives are reached.

It is not uncommon for leaders to have others in management positions responsible for accountability of resources and employee management. But, sometimes the leader him or herself will need to manage these (at least certain aspects). For example, a leader may need to manage (oversee) the overall financial stability of the organization. Or, the leader may find it necessary to manage certain staff due to their roles in the organization (perhaps as direct reports).

Knowing how to manage can be the result of various mechanisms. It is up to the leader to make sure this skill is apparent. For some leaders, a combination of leadership and management skills has been acquired over time based on varying professional experiences. Others, however, may need to take management courses to help them gain the appropriate skillset.

There are many contributing factors towards knowing how to manage. One of the most important is determining the appropriate management technique or model for a given situation. Leadership with an emphasis on talent development, for example, might be more inclined towards developmental management techniques that include aspects of behavioral analysis. On the other hand, leaders with a specific purpose to reach a certain goal may be more interested in management models directly aimed at achieving objectives.

It might be said, there is a fine line between leading and managing. Without a doubt, there are clear distinctions between leadership and management. It seems, all too often, some leaders lack in management skills necessary for their particular area of leadership. Nonetheless, leaders with a combination of leadership and management skills (i.e., leaders who know how to manage) can be powerful.

IDEA #18: EXPRESSES APPRECIATION

Amazingly, sometimes the easiest thing to do is the very thing that does not happen. For instance, saying "thank you". It is really a privilege to be a true leader. In turn, it is a pleasure to be able to show appreciation to others. The simple, impactful, yet often overlooked, act of conveying the message of thankfulness to others is paramount to effective leadership. A leader who regularly demonstrates gratitude to others is in many ways an emerging leader.

Considering most people are desirous of being shown appreciation, it should be acknowledged that this is not too much to ask for from leadership. Ironically, most leaders want to be appreciated. Therefore, it is unseemly for those in leadership positions to choose to refrain from conveying likewise sentiments to others. When leaders' express appreciation, it communicates to the organization that thankfulness is expected. Expressions of gratitude tend to become the norm throughout the organization. Consequently, a more positive and uplifting atmosphere is likely to surface.

Leaders who frequently express appreciation when employees, for example, produce high quality products are likely to see a continuance of such efforts. Sincere appreciation can make a person want to be more productive, excel more than previously and produce better results. Moreover, people tend to have a better attitude, be more personable, behave appropriately and have a better outlook of the organization when they are valued. These benefits to the organization are remarkable.

So, clearly, leadership that expresses appreciation is leadership that respects its employees and all other stakeholders. More emergent leaders of this kind are needed. They can be the hallmark of a thriving society. This type of leadership can transcend most expectations.

IDEA #19: ADMONISHES GOSSIP

It takes special people, perhaps, to be able to avoid gossip. Leaders need to admonish gossip at all times. Gossip can be toxic to an organization. Unfortunately, gossipers can be found in even the best organizations.

Of course, as human beings we are compelled to communicate with one another. This is needed and expected. However, communication in the form of gossip is unnecessary. Gossipers tend to seek attention. They may have a desire to be liked or noticed. Sadly, they go about fulfilling these "so-called needs" by intentionally speaking wrongly about others. It takes profound leadership skills to be able to remove gossiping from an organization. At least, an effort to minimize gossiping should be sought.

One way for leaders to rid the organization of gossiping is to approach the matter directly with employees. The leader might consider written communication, for example, that specifically calls for an end to the unprofessionalism of gossiping. The message may include examples of scenarios which showcase how gossiping can be disruptive to the work flow. It might also indicate the effects of gossiping on colleagues.

Failure to address the negative act of gossiping in the workplace is tantamount to encouraging an environment of lies and deceit. In the form of incorrect information, erroneous content or blatant faulty dialogue, gossip is pathetic.

Leadership will not allow gossip to permeate the organization. Rather, leadership will address the issue head-on. When leaders admonish gossip they encourage an atmosphere of honesty, integrity and respect. Undoubtedly, this is the type of environment in which most employees, if not all, would prefer to be a part of. Leaders need to take the lead against gossip.

IDEA #20: BOTTOM LINE CONSCIOUS

Believe it or not, leadership should be fully aware of the bottom line. In the minds of some, it is almost as if it is taboo to be bottom line conscious. This type of thinking is nonsensical. Leaders who are cognizant of the bottom line tend to be leaders who make better financial decisions. They also are more likely to make informed decisions in other areas which impact costs associated with the organization. Bottom line conscious can alleviate unnecessary concerns as well as address areas where changes are needed. Being bottom line conscious should be embraced, expected and encouraged. To do otherwise, is simply absurd.

Financial awareness, just like financial discussions, is not always the most fun of activities. It sometimes reveals the need for drastic changes. Other times it may indicate the necessity for making a few adjustments. Hopefully, however, it will let the leader know that all is well, financially. Leaders, certainly, want the best and most profitable bottom line possible. When the bottom line shows profitability (esp., extraordinary profitability), the leader can make decisions toward establishing a trend or continuing an existing trend. Equally important, leaders should endeavor to reward those responsible for the profitability. At all levels, in a myriad of ways, people contribute to the bottom line. The contributions will, of course, likely vary. As such, comparable rewards based on fair assessments, etc., established by the organization, should be given.

Bottom line conscious leaders are capable of leading the organization in a positive direction. Cognizant of the financial strength of the organization, leaders can make decisions that benefit the entire organization. Clearly, having a bottom line conscious mindset is not to be discouraged or demeaned. Rather, it is to be encouraged and celebrated.

IDEA #21: ENCOURAGES CUSTOMER DELIGHT

Sometimes we repeat statements that "sound" good, but are not necessarily accurate or even beneficial when thought-out. For example, this statement is *not* true: The customer is always right. Of course, we all know the customer (any customer) is not *always* right. It is obvious, when some people use this statement, they are implying employees should take on the attitude that the customer is right to help the employee empathize or sympathize with the customer. The idea is to make it easier for the employee to resolve the problem and satisfy the customer.

Leaders, and others in the organization, realize the customer is not always right. In some cases, sadly, the customer may be dishonest. At other times, the customer may be rightly dissatisfied but chooses an inappropriate way to convey this to an employee. Nonetheless, everyone in the organization has a duty and responsibility to behave professionally, including when dealing with customers. Customers are needed, and are important, to organizations. They should be treated kindly and respectfully.

Perhaps, there is a better approach for leaders to consider: Encourage customer delight (in the first place). Delighting the customer goes beyond mere satisfaction. It entails going above and beyond to initially please the customer with exceptional service and high-quality products. The beauty and significance of this approach is it has the capacity for displeased customers to be almost nonexistent. Leaders ought to contemplate adapting this method. Encouraging the organization to embrace customer delight may result in increased customers, higher customer retention, improved customer relations, more satisfied employees and a better overall organization.

IDEA #22: DRESS TO IMPRESS

In the workplace, appropriate attire is expected. Depending on the type of organization, the dress code may vary. However, leadership should encourage appropriate attire within the organization. In addition, leaders should dress to impress, as appropriate, too.

Without a doubt, outward appearance (i.e., apparel worn) is expected to be appropriate for the workplace. What is considered appropriate may vary depending on the type of organization and even the kind of work performed. Nonetheless, a leader should model appropriate attire at all times.

In some workplace environments, it is acceptable to dress casual on all or certain days. In others, expectations are for daily workday wear consisting of suits. Interestingly, however, it is typical for one in a leadership position to dress above casual attire. Leaders may need to attend meetings with others inside or outside the organization. Or, for example, leaders may need to conduct business interactions outside the confines of the office. Therefore, leaders tend to dress in appropriate business garb on a regular basis.

One's clothing can "say a lot about the person". Leaders need to represent themselves and the organization appropriately at all times. Of course, there are certainly occasions where leaders can dress casually. However, this should be done at the right time. For instance, when a leader participates in playing golf he or she would not dress in normal business office attire.

The importance of dressing to impress is based on the premise that outward appearance is an essential aspect of the organization. Potential clients or customers, for instance, may decide whether or not to do business with an organization based on the "professional look" of the employees and leadership. Professional appeal, based on appropriate attire, is important.

IDEA #23: RESOLVES TO CONTINUALLY IMPROVE

It should be the desire of a leader to continuously improve. There is no such thing, per se, as "having arrived" (i.e., no longer needing to improve). In one or more areas of life, everyone needs to continue to improve. Ideally, a leader will resolve to continually improve. This does not imply failing to be content or being satisfied with something. It simply means the leader recognizes there are certain areas that necessitate improvement. Those areas can be personal, professional and/or within the organization itself. Hence, leadership resolves to continually improve.

Amazingly, some people don't seem to truly comprehend the need for constant improvement. Some employees do not understand why they need to get better at completing certain tasks. Interestingly, some in leadership positions fail to recognize their need for improvement in how they interact with organizational stakeholders.

Leaders, undoubtedly, need to improve on a regular basis to sustain their leadership abilities. Without continuous improvement, a leader can become ineffective. The purpose of resolving to continuously improve rests upon the leader's recognition of the need for bettering self, others and the organization. This means the leader is interested in, for example, advances in knowledge. The leader is well aware that making a deliberate effort, on a regular basis, to make improvements requires a willingness to place such a desire as a priority. That is, it is not optional. Rather, it is a requirement to find areas where improvement is needed; and, take the necessary steps towards actual improvement. This process is continuous. Leaders who embrace the resolve to continually improve are more likely to overcome challenges and accomplish more. They will likely exemplify leadership with dedicated followers. It is perhaps easier to follow one who is passionate about continuously improving him or herself, others and the organization.

IDEA #24: EMBRACES CHANGE

In many ways, the word "change" seems to be overused. Change, for the sake of change, should not be the goal of a leader. Instead, leaders should embrace change that will result in specifically defined positive results. Pursuing the right kind of change can be difficult for those who lack leadership skills. The right change effort is based on the pursuit of making a transformation. The change, therefore, becomes a beacon for the ultimate goal: transformation.

Some organizations, unfortunately, include "change" in the mission and vision statements. But, there are no real efforts at truly defining what needs to be changed and why it needs to be changed. Again, it appears to be merely an attempt at including language to showcase the organization is in-tune with the need for, or value of, including some type of change—akin to the old adage of "change, for the sake of change".

When leadership embraces change from the perspective of making transformations, the leadership becomes impassioned about seeking where real change is needed. Moreover, leaders begin to harness ideas and approaches that will result in the positive transformations. Excitement transcends an organization where leadership embraces change that transforms. The excitement yields thought processes beyond mediocrity. When the transformation emerges it is a way for the organization to showcase the impact of real change. The leader is able to use the realized transformation as a means for the next change opportunity. One transformation success can make the way for successive transformation successes.

Making a change, just for the sake of change, is not necessarily useful or effective. It takes remarkable leadership to *identify* opportunities for change that transforms; and, actually make the opportunities for change that transforms into a *reality*.

IDEA #25: CONTEMPLATES AND THINKS BEFORE TAKING ACTION

It takes an awareness of what's important, coupled with maturity, to be able to contemplate and think prior to taking action. Leaders who can envision what is not yet realized, based on sound rationale, are able to ponder possibilities that may emerge in the future. With this insight, leaders can take the right actions. When a leader makes an effort to contemplate and think about issues affecting the organization, it is more likely the right actions on behalf of the organization will take place.

Real leadership requires the right foundation. A leader has a better chance of being able to visualize what is possible when the foundation for his or her thoughts is right. The basis for a leader's thoughts can dramatically impact what actions are pursued. To contemplate and think before actions are taken, a leader should ensure the root of the thought process is manifested in what is true. One way to do this is to ascertain if the thought-process mechanism makes sense, is established in reality, and is proven credible and reliable. When a leader is consistently able to contemplate and consider possibilities beyond what is current, the likelihood for taking the right action towards positive increases in the organization will more than likely result.

It may appear that this approach is rather easy to do. However, without the right foundation this approach is not likely to be fruitful. This suggests, then, leaders need to become aware of what is important, really important. Also, leaders need to be mature. Maturity is reflected in the ability to use sound reason as well as seek proven credible and reliable sources.

IDEA #26: DECISIVE

Leadership entails being decisive. Indecision is not the mark of leadership. Leaders know when a decision needs to be made; and, the leader makes the best decision possible. Given the situation and circumstances, leaders make every effort to gain as much truthful information, data and facts as possible. These are the precursor elements required for effective decision making. Upon evaluation and analysis of the aforementioned, a decision is made as quickly as possible. Leaders, of course, want to make the right decision in a reasonable amount of time. Real leaders are decisive.

Leaders need to be unwavering in their decisions. They need to make a decision and stick with it. This does not mean there can be no "tweaking" allowed. There are occasions when it is necessary to make adjustments, modifications or amendments. But, the overarching decision should remain.

Getting truthful information is essential for effective leadership. Sadly, some information is misinformation and some information is unnecessary or irrelevant. Truthful information is sought by leaders willing to make the right decisions. This type of information is real. It is genuine. As such, leaders should be interested in gaining truthful information from those who have proven themselves to be honest. Getting truthful information from those with integrity is essential to a real leader. Therefore, it befits leaders to have integrity themselves and to surround themselves with others who have integrity. Real leadership should rely on those with proven, impeccable, honor characteristics and a desire for uprightness.

Getting the right data and facts is also valuable towards being decisive. Leaders can be more certain they are making informed decisions when they are presented with, and make decisions based on, accurate data and facts. Leadership involves being resolute about the accuracy of data and facts. Real leaders do not want, nor have an acceptance for, inaccurate or misleading data and so-called "facts".

Decisive leaders are pivotal in organizations. They are the hallmark of the organization reflecting fundamentally the value of making timely, informed, decisions with certainty, based on truth and accurate data and facts.

IDEA #27: ACTIVE LISTENER

Communication skills are important at all levels of an organization. Important to note, though, is the need for leaders to be active listeners. All too often, people hear words. But, they do not internalize what they hear as part of the active listening process. Active listening means seeking to understand what is being conveyed without error. It requires minimizing, better yet refraining from, interrupting the speaker. Admittedly, there are times when it is necessary to interrupt someone who is speaking inappropriately, giving misleading information or when additional information is needed for the receiver to understand what was conveyed (prior to the message sender going forward with more content). Therefore, part of active listening is listening for appropriateness and accuracy of what is conveyed as well as comprehension.

Leaders who are active listeners tend to be able to hone in on what is intended to be conveyed by the message sender. Because they listen intently, they are better able to clearly understand what is communicated. Their level of comprehension is heightened, therefore. This is the key aspect of active listening.

Another important point about active listening is it is efficient. There is little to no need for repeating content over and over again. The active listener is cognizant of the message as intended early on. Consequently, leaders who are active listeners tend to be better equipped to make decisions in a timely manner.

It may take time and effort to become an active listener. Nonetheless, leaders should endeavor to be active listeners. The time and effort put forth to practice this skill is worthwhile.

IDEA #28: ENCOURAGES KNOWLEDGE SHARING

There are definite times when it is beneficial, as well as necessary, to share ideas or information with others. This is especially evident in the workplace. Of course, the concept of "need to know" must be adhered to, as well. As such, knowledge sharing is appropriate as long as there is a "need to know" basis. Leadership requires knowing *who* to share information with, *what* information to share, *when* to share such information, *where* or *how* to share the information and *why* it is necessary to share the information.

Ironically, there are some employees in the workplace who fail to understand the value and importance of encouraging appropriate knowledge sharing. It is as if they mistakenly believe that doing so will make them no longer valuable or needed in the workplace. This is where leadership is needed to explain and encourage knowledge sharing. Knowledge sharing is not about giving up leverage or one's importance, so to speak. Rather, it entails a clear understanding of the need to formulate processes and procedures that are efficient and effective. When knowledge is shared, it is much easier to create an operational management and leadership environment whereby essential tasks are completed timely and accurately.

Leadership embodies a willingness to share appropriate knowledge with others. Thus, hoarding of information, for one's own selfish reason, should be discouraged. Proper dissemination of information benefits the organization. Leaders, therefore, need to regularly encourage employees to share knowledge in an effort to streamline processes and procedures, where applicable. An organization where knowledge sharing is expected and embraced can be an organization where operations are improved or perhaps enhanced. Surely, a leader would want this type of organizational environment.

IDEA #29: INCORPORATES STRATEGIES TO ENCOURAGE EXCELLENCE IN CUSTOMER BEHAVIOR

Employee customer service is communicated in most organizations. However, it is also important to encourage customers to behave appropriately when they interact with employees at all levels. Leaders who comprehend the necessity and significance of incorporating strategies to this end are perhaps more likely to have positive organizational environments. When employees constantly have to deal with customers who display poor behavior, this can cause employees to become disgruntled and have a negative effect on employee retention. Leaders who take the time to address this issue can dramatically change, in a positive way, the organization.

First, leadership must be willing to put to rest the misnomer that "the customer is *always* right". No human being is always right. Next, leadership must consider strategies to employ to encourage customers to approach employees in an appropriate manner. For example, a sign at the entrance to the organization that reads something like the following may be one idea: "If there is a problem, be calm and respectful as you notify us. We will go above and beyond to help you. We will seek resolutions to your satisfaction." Proper behavior by customers can make it easier for employees to address customers' concerns in a timely manner and to the customers' satisfaction. Why? Because the employee is able to think better and thus consider available options and the best solution. So, the customer benefits and the employee benefits from calm and respectful behavior from customers. As an added benefit to the organization, when the employee is able to resolve the situation due to being able to think clearly in a calm environment, it is less likely for a manager or leader to need to step in to address the issue. This is reflective of true employee empowerment. Not to mention, no longer needing to "go up the chain of command" to be able to address customers' concerns allows those in middle or senior level positions to be able to complete more workplace tasks and responsibilities without distractions or interruptions.

IDEA #30: KNOW HOW TO SUPERVISE

Amazingly, people are put into leadership positions without any real experience or knowledge of how to supervise, manage or lead others. This is actually quite troubling. This lack of experience and knowledge can lead to poor productivity results as well as an ineffective culture in the workplace. It is, therefore, helpful for leaders to have experience and knowledge of supervision.

One way to help ensure leaders have the appropriate experience is to provide opportunities to move up in the organization. In some organizations, those in leadership positions have learned and gained valuable experience as a result of being in the organization in various roles. These roles allow the individuals to have exposure to the challenges associated with being in a leadership role.

Also, promotional opportunities within the organization can allow individuals to learn various tasks including how to handle certain situations. Increases in job responsibilities, therefore, allow individuals who will move into leadership positions the opportunity to learn and grow (i.e., become more knowledgeable) as well as hone in on leadership characteristics, such as supervision.

Supervising others, as a part of leadership, is an essential skill. At some point or another, a leader will need to supervise one or more employees directly. As such, knowing how to effectively supervise will allow the leader to be more effective in this role. In addition to being more effective, the leader will be more equipped to positively transform the organization, make the right decisions and help others toward leadership positions when he or she is able to effectively supervise others.

IDEA #31: RESPONSIBLE AND ACCOUNTABLE

To be in a leadership position is truly a privilege. As such, it is necessary to exercise responsibility and accountability in one's actions at all times. Doing so encourages and motivates others in the organization to do the same. This can positively impact the norms of the organization yielding an atmosphere where ethical behavior is likely to be clearly evident.

A leader who embraces responsibility and accountability is needed in today's society, just like ethical behavior is needed. Leadership is not merely a word with no meaning and impact. Rather, leadership itself (to those who truly understand what leadership represents) is indicative of doing one's best to be responsible and accountable. Sadly, and perhaps all too often, some in leadership positions do not comprehend the real meaning of being a leader. Moreover, the impact of this lack of comprehension is clearly seen in organizations where leadership has resulted in poor decisions.

When making decisions, a leader needs to be able to convey to others (esp., those affected by the decision) the rationale for the decision. Of course, credible and reliable information, as well as proven facts, should be essential elements to the decisions that are made. Others in the organization are more likely to be ethical and have confidence in leadership when the leader consistently demonstrates an attitude of being responsible and accountable.

Without a doubt, it takes maturity and character to be willing to be responsible and accountable. Leaders with maturity and character can seize the opportunity to positively impact their organizations with a workplace environment where ethical behavior is likely to be the norm.

IDEA #32: ABLE TO ARTICULATE HONEST IDEAS TO OTHERS

Some people believe a leader needs to be charismatic to be effective. While this may be appealing to some, to others it is more of a distraction. Using charisma to get others to follow a leader will not be sustaining if the leader's message is deemed ineffective or dishonest. On the other hand, a leader who is able to articulate ideas to others that are truthful can more likely encourage others to accept the ideas conveyed. This is to say, for example, if you asked people which do they prefer, a charismatic person in a leadership position who regularly conveys untruths or a non-charismatic person in a leadership position who regularly conveys the truth, it is likely they would choose the latter.

Whether it is outwardly expressed or not, most people prefer a leader who is authentic, honest and displays integrity. No one, from a common-sense viewpoint, would purposely want someone in a leadership position who cannot be trusted to provide the truth.

Leaders who value the importance of being able to articulate honest ideas to others are exceptional. They will tend to be less self-serving and more interested in doing what is right and in the best interest of others. To be able to do what is right, a leader has to desire to be honest with those he or she leads. Of course, there are occasions where a "need to know" situation may exist for various reasons. Nonetheless, real leaders want to be upfront with others.

Having the mindset and heart to be a person of integrity and to be honest with others is a needed character trait of a leader. Leaders who constantly demonstrate an attitude and temperament representative of doing what's right helps towards making better and more effective decisions. Others tend to be more receptive to decisions made by a leader when those decisions are based on honesty. This is why it is beneficial to have leaders who are able to articulate honest ideas to others.

IDEA #33: CLEARLY CONVEYS
THE MISSION AND VISION

It really takes an effective leader to be able to clearly convey the mission and vision. Both need to be articulated in a manner whereby there is no confusion or misunderstanding. That is, the mission and vision statements should be easy to comprehend. This, of course, also presumes the mission and vision make sense and are achievable.

Undoubtedly, the mission requires acknowledging there are essential goals and objectives to be met. As such, the overarching mission established by a leader necessitates a qualified team to carry out the mission. Ideally, the purpose of the mission, and the mission itself, should be clear and concise. Sometimes, the purpose for the mission is not completely understood by some in the organization. There can be a multitude of reasons for this; but, probably, it is due to a lack of understanding as to what is important for the organization to be successful. Understanding the need for the mission is just as important as comprehension of the actual mission. Leaders need to be able to explain both succinctly.

There is simply no denying a leader needs to be visionary. Certainly, leaders are responsible for the present (current time), in terms of effectively leading their organizations. Moreover, leaders need to be knowledgeable of the past (historical time). But, it is vitally important for a leader to be hopeful for the future (upcoming time).

Ensuring daily objectives are accomplished is a key factor for effective leadership. Job-related tasks need to be completed regularly (perhaps daily). Therefore, a leader who understands the importance of "today" recognizes this as a way to ensure continuity of important actions. However, it is beneficial in numerous ways for leaders to be mindful of history. A leader who is interested in historical facts (i.e., based on proven credible and reliable sources) can make a tremendous impact on an organization; thus, having the ability to lead it in a positive manner with profound integrity. Because the leader is aware of what works and what does not work (historically speaking), the leader can make better, more informed, decisions. Furthermore, a leader who has a vision can significantly transform an organization into one that positively affects all stakeholders. Considerations of "what can be" or "what is possible" reflects a leader who has aspirations for the betterment of the organization. A leader who is a visionary can motivate others towards "buy in" to the vision. The vision should be simple to explain yet powerful enough to spark excitement.

A leader who effectively and consistently communicates the mission and vision is one who is likely to ensure the outcome of both. In many ways, the mission and vision are complementary. A mission without a vision will ensure daily tasks are completed; however, innovation, creativity and major improvements are unlikely. A vision without a mission is akin to wishful thinking that is unlikely to result in the fruition of a desired major and impactful change. However, a mission with a vision takes into account aspects associated with accomplishing tasks in an effort towards determining to make drastic transformations. That is to say, when a leader is able to establish a mission coupled with a vision, and is actively determined to ensure both are realized, the leader is determined to take the organization from a likely acceptable state to an extraordinary entity. To begin to do this, a leader needs to convey the mission and vision clearly.

IDEA #34: YES MEANS YES; AND NO MEANS NO

A leader must have standards to be successful. In this context, success is meant to refer to that which makes a positive impact on others for their long-term (albeit, lifelong) betterment. Moreover, a leader should expect more of himself or herself to be able to set a positive example. The aforementioned suggests a leader should be able to have words that are believable. Stated differently, a leader's words should be based on what he or she will do. A real leader says what he or she means and means what he or she says. To put it bluntly, a real leader is interested in, and actively pursues, being truthful. This does not mean a leader cannot change his or her mind. Rather, it expresses the importance for the leader to be one of integrity. So, when a leader says, "Yes", this is what is meant. When a leader says, "No", this is what is meant. Yes does not mean no; and, no does not mean yes (Note: So-called leaders who display this trait of confusion will ultimately be viewed as failures as well as manipulative and deceptive. They are not trustworthy). Real leaders truly want to mean what they say.

Leadership based on "mean what you say" is sorely needed. Employees need to be able to trust the leader. If there is no trust, which goes both ways by the way, there is likely to be minimal effort, low productivity levels, below average (or at most average) performance, inattentiveness to ethical behavior, little to no demonstration of morals or values in the workplace, minimization of critical thought associated with completion of job tasks, little to no desire for innovativeness and creativity, and/or low levels of satisfactory customer service.

Leaders who do not follow the "mean what you say" approach to effective leadership will certainly create a toxic environment where employees at all levels will likely experience burnout and abhor going to work. The atmosphere will likely be one that is pitiful, miserable and quite frankly unbecoming. To counter such an atmosphere, it will take drastic change evidenced by an effective leader coming on board who embraces "mean what you say". That is, a leader who epitomizes "yes means yes; and no means no".

IDEA #35: ASSERTIVE WITHOUT BEING OVERBEARING

An assertive leader is firm, fair and considerate of others. This type of leader is not interested in being overbearing. Leaders who are assertive tend to be respected. Conversely, those in leadership positions who are overbearing are more likely to not be respected (even if it is not outwardly conveyed). These so-called leaders tend to demand respect, based on their actions, words and/or overall behavior. It is fascinating, however, that real leaders do not have to demand respect. It is *naturally* given to them because of their character. Interesting, huh!

When an assertive leader is firm, there is the tendency for expectations to be clearly expressed. Moreover, communication is much more likely to be two-way, consistent and appreciated. When employees are aware of the leader's expectations, it is easier for them to ensure those expectations are met. Simply put, expectations should be clear, concise and understandable.

An assertive leader, in terms of being fair, will make it a point to do what is right on a regular basis. This leader can admit mistakes or being wrong. Obviously, no one human-being is 100% correct 100% of the time. So, it is not surprising when one makes a mistake. As such, leaders can, and will, make mistakes, too. However, a leader of profound character is willing and able to admit mistakes or being wrong.

When a leader is considerate of others, his or her assertiveness is illustrated. It takes a stable person to desire being considerate of others. A clear representation of consideration for others is when, for instance, the leader puts others before himself or herself on a consistent basis.

IDEA #36: COURAGEOUS

Real leaders are courageous. They do not shy away from making decisions based on what is right. Rather, they embrace the opportunity to do what is right even if others are not interested in doing so. Their courage is likened to a dove and a lion. Like the eloquence of a dove, they model the right behavior in a classy manner. At the same time, like the fearlessness of a lion, they stand up to those who purposely, directly or indirectly, purport ill-intentions.

Courageous leadership is seen by those who, to be quite frank, abhor evil and wickedness. Interestingly, courageous leaders do not make it a point to take the credit for their courage. Rather, they understand that it comes from within. This understanding is essential because leaders of this caliber are uniquely designed and qualified to be in leadership positions. It is like they were created, or born, to be leaders at a given point in time. Intellectually, the aforementioned makes complete sense (esp., when one understands there is a purpose for everything).

Remarkably, leaders who are brave have an uncanny ability to be self-less and genuinely care for others. They don't pretend to care. Their actions clearly demonstrate they really do care for others well-being. So, when tough or challenging decisions have to made, for the betterment of others, these leaders intentionally take the lead to persuade others of the importance of doing what is right (even if it means little to no recognition for the leader).

A fascinating aspect of courageous leaders is their comprehension of the task at hand. They enact what is best, despite opposition, for they have a keen awareness of the long-term benefits of their decisions. Moreover, they realize that it takes time for some people to see the light. So, they will do what is right, and in the best interest of others, even if they do not get immediate credit for it. These courageous leaders know that history will prove they were right. But, more importantly, they know that the courage to do what is right is a reward in and of itself.

IDEA #37: KIND-HEARTED

It is amazing that some people erroneously believe that kindness is a weakness. This could not be farther from the truth. It takes strength, that some people cannot comprehend, to choose to be kind-hearted. Anybody can be mean-spirited towards others. It does not take too much effort to do so. But, it takes an indescribable strength, beyond oneself, to be kind-hearted to others (esp., when it is human-nature to focus on oneself and one's desires). In essence, kind-hearted leaders are not self-absorbed or self-focused to the extent that they remove concern for others.

True leadership requires kind-heartedness. Leaders have followers; and, followers want the leader to show genuine kindness. Just think... what follower do you know that purposely wants a leader who is mean, rude, disrespectful, and the like? Without a doubt, it would be senseless to want an uncaring, non-compassionate, and unkind leader. But, again, the leader must be *genuinely* kind-hearted. It only takes a matter of time to determine the authenticity of the leader's kind-heartedness.

Of course, to be kind-hearted does not mean to be a push-over. Real leaders do not exhibit, nor expect others to exhibit, being a push-over. In fact, these leaders respect the value of being kind-hearted in that it represents having self-control while in authority. Having power, coupled with being kind-hearted (esp., to those who do not reciprocate kindness), is astonishing to behold. It is like the wonder of the Creator of human-beings (i.e., God) and His love for His creation (without *forcing* His creation on earth to love Him back). He has *all* the power, yet He also has love for human-beings and the willingness to let human-beings choose to love Him or not. Astonishing!

Leaders like this are more likely to have followers who themselves will aspire to model the leader's behavior. When this occurs, it represents the ultimate victory of real, true, authentic leadership: The emergence of other leaders (successors) who model the profound character and behavior of the leader.

IDEA #38: HAS BOTH KNOWLEDGE AND WISDOM

There are a lot of people with knowledge. But, there are few, in comparison, with wisdom. Leadership requires both to excel. All of the knowledge in the world is meaningless if not coupled with wisdom. Knowing something can be considered rather "typical"; however, being able to correctly apply knowledge to make people's lives better takes wisdom. For example, one can be knowledgeable about concepts associated with leadership. Yet, this knowledge alone is not sufficient. It takes the ability to actually correctly apply knowledge gained to transform the lives of others in a positive manner (or, to make a positive impact on the lives of others) to reflect real leadership. That is, it takes wisdom to garner positive transformations. It is important to note, wisdom comes from beyond oneself. Its source is, and can only be, the source of all truth (i.e., the source of all that is correct): God!

This implies, therefore, a leader cannot truly (i.e., without fail at any point) apply knowledge to make positive transformations on his or her own. Hence, the leader will be inclined to give credit where it is due. To put it another way, leaders with knowledge and wisdom will refrain from use, or overuse of: I, me and my. They will not puff themselves up. Quite the contrary, these leaders will acknowledge the source of the wisdom given to them.

Suffice it to say, many have knowledge; but, few have wisdom. Leaders need both. Having knowledge reflects a level of understanding or comprehension, which is important. Having wisdom reveals knowing what to do, coupled with knowledge, to make accurate decisions. This is not only important but very much *needed*.

A person in a leadership position who has knowledge, but lacks wisdom, isn't really a leader. This person has some level of understanding but may not necessarily have the ability to make correct decisions. However, it is possible to be a leader who lacks certain knowledge, yet has wisdom. This person may require more knowledge to have a better understanding but it does not prevent the leader from being able to make accurate decisions. Since the wisdom given to the leader is from the ultimate source of truth and what is correct (God), the leader uses the wisdom to make precisely the right decision. In essence, the correct answer is given to the leader. Overtime, however, the leader will endeavor to increase knowledge in certain areas which can be considered normal human nature.

IDEA #39: FEARS GOD

Understanding the importance of fearing God is an aspect of leadership that some (perhaps many) people do not adequately comprehend. To fear God is to rightly understand who He is and to accept Him as Lord. Both are essential. Leadership, then, requires acknowledgement of one's limitations and placement of one's trust in God.

When a leader fears God, there is a reverence for God. To revere the Lord demonstrates respect for Him. For example, God is the creator of all. There is none above the Lord. No one can compare to God's greatness and excellency. It takes a humble leader to fear God. Arrogance, pride and being egotistic are not in line with a healthy fear of God. Humility, as a character trait of a leader based on a fear of God, emphasizes one's willingness to express appreciation for what is above. To do otherwise is counterintuitive to humbleness.

Accepting God as Lord, in one sense, is to acknowledge and desire God's will as being more important than the leader's will or any other person's will. Unfortunately, there are some people in leadership positions who are not interested in the *perfect* will of God. Rather, they are interested in doing things their own way or in a way that pleases another man or woman (even if it is clearly wrong to do so). Real leaders know that it makes complete sense to desire and do the will of God. Since God's will is perfect, this is what a real leader will want. Leadership, at its best, is keen on being the most productive with the highest level of integrity and demonstration of the highest standards. It takes an honest and faithful relationship with God, for instance, on a consistent and regular basis, to accomplish the aforementioned. This does not imply a leader will not make mistakes. A human-being, who is allowed to be a leader, is not perfect. God is the One who *is* perfect. Due to the imperfection of human-beings, God is needed in our lives. When a leader does what God commands and directs him or her to do, God's will (desire) makes the outcome the best.

Every leader has limitations. No human-being who is a leader is exempt. But, the leader who puts trust in God is the one who can overcome those limitations. That is, this type of leader will discourage emphasis on self and encourage emphasis on the Lord. Put another way, leadership should strive to reduce or minimize selfishness and increase or maximize selflessness. Selfishness puts the importance on oneself; whereas, selflessness is a reflection of importance on others (most importantly, importance on God).

IDEA #40: ENCOURAGES DIVERSITY OF THOUGHT (INDIVIDUAL THOUGHT: THINKING FOR ONESELF)

There are some words that, at certain times, tend to come up quite often. Today, one of those words is *diversity*. However, interestingly, "diversity of thought" is not given as much attention as it should. To "think for oneself" is to be interested in the truth and what is right. Thinking for oneself is a way to show interest in getting to the heart of the matter. When this is genuine, as it should be, there is little interest in mere dialogue, debate or discussion. Of course, there are times when it is helpful, and perhaps even necessary, to engage in dialogues, debates and discussions. However, these can be meaningless if they do not lead to discovery of truth and actions that reflect what is right. For this reason, it is useful for leaders to encourage diversity of thought, with the premise of seeking the truth and what is right. Leaders who encourage others this way are more likely to be interested in the truth and what is right themselves. Thus, this can become the norm in the organization or setting.

A leader who understands the value of diversity of thought is one who typically has a high level of self-esteem. It takes profound confidence and integrity to be able to motivate others toward an atmosphere where diversity of thought is embraced. When others (e.g., followers) view their ideas and suggestions as taken seriously, they will be more inclined to think, ponder, rationalize, etc. In essence, they are more likely to engage in deliberate thought processes towards the best solutions for resolving issues and solving problems. This is the kind of information that can be shared with the leader to help him or her make informed decisions.

Whether it is directly conveyed or not, people (esp., mature adults) really do want to think for themselves. They do not want to be puppets. Regurgitating the thoughts of others, without being able to have some input, will likely become boring over time. It does not take talents, skills or abilities to merely repeat what someone wants you to say. Yet, it does take talents, skills or abilities to be able to think for oneself (e.g., to think outside the box) and be part of the decision-making process (e.g., in terms of sharing meaningful ideas).

Therefore, a leader needs a team of individuals that are motivated to think for themselves while simultaneously being interested in meeting the teams' desired goals. Clearly, a high level of leadership expertise is necessary to be able to inspire individual thought.

IDEA #41: PROBLEM-SOLVER

Most would agree, leaders need to be problem-solvers. Rhetoric is not enough. Leadership necessitates being able to take purposeful action to make things better. Solving problems, resolving issues and addressing concerns, require leaders who not only have the skill-set to do so, but more importantly have the heart (i.e., passion) to do so.

Some people in leadership positions may have some skills, but they lack the passion to make things better. Perhaps it is their own self-serving interests that prevent them from having the heart to truly make things better for others. Or, maybe, it is a lack of genuine compassion for others which prevents them from being interested in making things better for other people. Those in leadership positions who may have certain skillsets, but lack the heart (passion) to solve problems, resolve issues and address concerns to make things better, are really ill-equipped to be effective leaders.

Leaders who are passionate about being problem-solvers are, in some ways, rather unique. It is not too often that people, in general, indicate a desire to regularly address concerns and resolve issues. Leadership, however, typically has to solve problems on an on-going basis. Since leaders continuously need to make things better and constantly improve, problem-solving is a must.

Of course, leaders can, and should, get feedback from others. However, ultimately, the leader has to make the right decision to solve the problem. Any decision won't do...it has to be the *right* decision. There are occasions when the leader will have substantial time to contemplate the best way to resolve the issue. In other situations, the leader may have limited time available before a decision has to be made. The key, regardless of the allotted time, is for the leader to be a problem-solver and make the best decision for the desired outcome. Being a problem-solver is an essential component of being an effective leader.

IDEA #42: HAS CONFLICT RESOLUTION SKILLS

Being able to solve problems, resolve issues, and quite frankly improve situations, takes leadership. Therefore, leaders need to have conflict resolution skills. Interestingly, managing conflict need not be difficult. Key factors are the leader's listening skills, interpersonal skills and commitment to be a problem solver.

It is amazing how many problems, issues and negative situations go unresolved. It is almost as if some people intentionally prefer such havoc. But, effective leaders understand the value of resolving matters of conflict. Therefore, they take the time to listen. When conflicts emerge, leaders really need to be active listeners. They need to be engaged in conversations or discussions to the point where they truly understand what is the real, foundational, problem. Often, it seems as if the real issue (root) is never discovered. Rather, time is wasted on other factors (branches or leaves) that are the result of the real issue (root). Active listening promotes an interest in getting the *beneath the surface* realities.

For leaders to be able to gain knowledge about the root of the problem, active listening needs to be coupled with having interpersonal skills. Leaders need to be interested in people. Meaning, they should be willing to be attentive to the needs of others. Moreover, there is the need for leaders to be involved in the completion of job-related tasks (esp., important ones), as much as possible, with their followers.

A leader can have great interpersonal skills and be an active listener; however, if the leader does not sincerely commit to being a problem solver, conflicts will not likely be resolved. This commitment needs to be reflective of the leader, as well as the organizational environment, and be an established norm. That said, effective leadership has an acute awareness of the importance of conflict resolution. In addition, effective leaders know quite well the value of having conflict resolution (problem-solving) permeate throughout the organization. In essence, everyone at all levels should have a mindset for improving situations for better functionality of the overall organization.

Of course, it is how you view things that matters. For example, conflicts can be viewed as opportunities. This is one reason why it should saturate the entire organization. Without a doubt, there will be conflicts (e.g., differences and disagreements). But, when viewed as opportunities, those conflicts that materialize can be used to produce undiscovered and extraordinary outcomes which in turn transform the organization. Since conflicts cannot be circumvented entirely, it makes sense to embrace them as opportunities for improvement.

Leaders, of course, want as much improvement as possible and on a continuous basis. Therefore, effective leaders will want some level of involvement (directly or indirectly) with ensuring problems are solved, issues are resolved and situations are improved. Realistically, though, leaders cannot be everywhere at all times. So, there are certainly occasions when they will have to delegate others to resolve conflicts. They are human-beings so it is impossible for them to be omni-present.

IDEA #43: AVOIDS FOOLISHNESS

For some leaders, "foolishness" might be a pet-peeve. Thus, it necessitates doing this regularly: Avoiding foolishness. Not surprisingly, foolishness, if allowed, can drag down an entity. If one is to be honest, sadly there are times when some situations are just *ridiculous*. I am sure many will agree. To better articulate this, however, let's say there are occasions when a leader has to deal with senseless situations. Ask any real leader if they have ever had to deal with situations that were meaningless (and a waste of time) and you are more likely than not to receive an answer such as, "Of course, who hasn't".

To be blunt, leaders unfortunately find themselves dealing with absurdity all too often. For the aspiring leader, as well as the seasoned leader, it is important to know how to curtail all acts of, or situations reflecting, foolishness. To begin, have a perspective whereby foolishness is neither acceptable nor allowed to linger. That is, if a foolish situation presents itself, it should be addressed with a sense of urgency (i.e., immediately). Otherwise, it could bring about a negative connotation that exacerbates the situation. This is where effective leadership shines. The leader will make it a point to have irrationalities dealt with quickly. Pointless discussions, too, will be discontinued. Discussions can be revisited at a later time when those involved are willing to bring rational ideas to the table.

Avoiding foolishness is necessary esp. involving situations of importance. Foolishness is akin to wasting time. This is to say, it can be likened to purposeful derailing of effective communications. So, clearly, leaders should avoid, dismiss, refuse to engage in, and reduce the impact of foolishness.

Successful leaders know how to take foolishness and turn it into thoughtful, rational and logical results. Being able to do so takes a leader who is results-oriented. Leaders who focus on producing results do not have time for activities that waste time or are foolish. Rather, they seek ways to turn the foolishness into activities that drive high, sustainable, long-lasting solutions. Interestingly, it may take time to find such solutions. However, the leader will prefer to maximize his or her efforts towards those solutions versus spending useless time on foolishness.

IDEA #44: HOLISTIC AWARENESS (BIG PICTURE VIEW)

While it is definitely necessary and beneficial for leaders to analyze varying aspects of the organization, for instance, it is also important to take a holistic view. Leadership may be able to gain more insight by having holistic awareness—getting a big picture view. This kind of awareness allows the leader to truly internalize what is occurring in the organization. A big picture vantage point provides a leader with an overall sense of what is being conveyed. Typically, for instance, followers will report on parts of the organization based on their role in it. This is understandable and to be expected. The leader, nonetheless, has to take these different parts and formulate a picture (i.e., representation) that captures all types of elements, including: small and big; minute and stark; or, insignificant and important. Once the depiction is clear to the leader, it is easier to envision the steps necessary to make the picture more captivating. Thus, the leader is ready to transform the organization into a more fascinating (albeit, successful) entity.

Leaders should desire to have a holistic awareness. But, they need time to do so. Effective leadership requires countless hours of time spent really understanding what is occurring in the organization at a deep, below-the-surface level and how to create a vision for the future. Many times a leader is overwhelmed with other occupational duties and responsibilities further minimizing available time. Therefore, it becomes challenging to garner a truly big picture view.

Regardless of the challenges, however, a real leader will allocate time to having a holistic awareness. In the long run, this effort has the propensity to lead to remarkable outcomes for the organization and its stakeholders. It is almost as if the leader's determination towards getting a big picture view may lead to an astounding return on investment (ROI). Perhaps, then, this is a strategy or strategic measure that leaders should undertake as soon as possible.

Of course, a holistic awareness or big picture view is not synonymous with the leader becoming omniscient. The leader is incapable of having complete knowledge. However, when leaders increase their knowledge, understanding (comprehension) and insight, they are better equipped to make the right decisions consistently.

As such, the investment in time necessary to achieve a big picture view should be considered by leaders. Optimistically, time afforded to holistic awareness will prove to be a wise investment.

IDEA #45: CREATIVE

Is it possible to be a leader without being creative? Some people might argue "yes". Others may say "no". A better question to ask might be: "What does it mean to be creative?"

In the context herein, being creative means to have the ability to think innovatively. Leaders who have fresh ideas can help in the achievement of seemingly impossible goals. Thus, leadership capabilities can perhaps be expanded by the leader regularly searching for fresh ideas (being creative).

This might seem strange, but in reality human beings do not *create* anything. One might interject that the term "create" is used quite loosely. Rather, as humans, we take something already in existence and change it in some way such that something different emerges. In the majority of situations, it seems, more than one thing is used to make something different.

As a leader, then, fresh ideas come from ideas that already existed and are changed in some way. Based on this statement, one can surmise that it is possible to *learn* to be creative. One way to do so is to take time on a regular basis (e.g., weekly or monthly) to ponder how to change something or some things into something entirely different; the ultimate goal of which should be for it to be useful for a beneficial and good purpose. Put another way, think beyond the obvious. Become a boundless thinker. Strive towards constructing ideas and objects to serve others in a positive and meaningful way.

In many ways, real leadership is about finding ways to better serve others (e.g., employees, customers, clients, stockholders, etc.). At an ultimate level, excellence in leadership is displayed when a leader is able to better serve all stakeholders (esp., simultaneously). So, is it possible to be a leader without being creative? Maybe. But, is it possible to be an *effective* (*great*) leader without being creative? Think about it!

IDEA #46: SENSE OF TIME

The concept of time is interesting. It seems as if there is never enough time to accomplish tasks. In some cases, time eludes us. Time just keeps going and going. People try to manage time and rightly so. Yet, perchance, time really is managing us. Leaders need to have a sense of time. Having intelligence about time can help a leader exercise more thoughtful decisions. Perceptions about time may differ; however, this is clear: Time is an unseen "commodity" that is best used when common sense is applied.

Leaders tend to be busy most of the time. Although it is necessary to ensure some tasks are accomplished, there are other tasks that simply are not important (at least at a particular moment). Leadership entails being able to utilize time to one's advantage. Being able to prioritize tasks is very helpful in this endeavor. Assigning a specific amount of time to certain tasks is useful, too. Possibly even more important, is having the wherewithal to be able to emphatically say "no" or "no, not at this time" to others, esp. when it is not feasible to do what is asked due to time constraints. Leaders who are mindful of time will most likely make the most effective decisions.

The concept of time and making decisions go hand-in-hand. Each moment of time, a decision is made as to what to do at that moment. Leaders who understand this try to make the best use of time by using it in a productive manner. For example, meetings and other activities should have designated timeframes established and adhered to. If it is necessary to revisit discussion items, this can be done at another appropriate time. For some leaders, one preferable approach is having predetermined time intervals (i.e., a schedule) throughout the day for completing activities. Other leaders may want and need a different approach with a more open plan allowing for unexpected events (e.g., unscheduled sessions with other leaders). A third approach, which is likely the most common, is a combination of both approaches.

As opposed to viewing time as something that is a disadvantage, it is better and more practical to view time as advantageous. This means, for instance, acknowledging there are 24 hours in a day; and, a certain amount of them can be used for making positive impacts during the work day, etc. Such approach puts time "on your side" and lends to a more proactive stance about time. A leader who embraces this approach may begin to find time as more than adequate (and, perhaps even, *just right*).

Leaders who have a sense of time will find methods to use to make time work for them. To do otherwise would have time working against them. Time is a key to effective decision-making; so, leaders should determine to view time from a positive perspective. Leadership is reflective of a commitment to ensuring things get done. Time is a component that allows leaders to monitor when it is necessary to prioritize certain activities. Suffice it to say, having a sense of time can help leaders excel in their role.

IDEA #47: DOES THE UNEXPECTED

One of the most profound character traits of a real leader is willing to do the unexpected. Jesus Christ, the *greatest, unmatched* and *perfect* leader, washed the disciples' feet (see St. John 13:5). Leaders of this caliber do kind acts that are unexpected because they genuinely understand leadership. Leadership reflects service. Real leaders *serve!* More specifically, real leaders serve in an impeccable way demonstrating service to others marked by doing what is right. They are not interested in self-serving ambitions that result in negative situations for others. Rather, they embody consistent acts of selflessness, putting others ahead of themselves with the understanding that doing so ultimately benefits them, too. These real leaders do the unexpected!

What does it take for a leader to be a blessing to others on a regular basis? If you were to pose this open-ended question to 100 people, many different responses would emerge. However, if you were to ask a more closed-ended question, such as: Is it "natural" for a leader to put others ahead of him- or her-self, you would easily likely get a simple "yes" or "no". The answers to the two questions might suggest, and be summarized to reflect: There are a variety of ways in which leaders can continuously do something beneficial in service to others. However, expectations, of astonishing behavior from leaders, are probably low. Hence, the value of leadership doing the unexpected is profound.

Imagine seeing a leader pick up trash (e.g., a piece of paper rolled up) lying in the middle of an office room and placing it in a nearby trash can. As simple as this gesture would be, how many leaders would actually do this? For that matter, how many people in general would do it? Is it likely most people would see the rolled-up piece of paper and ignore it?

When a leader does the unexpected, others are encouraged to exhibit the behavior, too. Overtime, it (doing the unexpected for the benefit of others) becomes behavior that is modeled throughout the organization. When this occurs, internal customers benefit, external customers benefit, etc. Improvements are likely to be evident: More positive attitudes; the organizational environment becomes more pleasant; productivity increases; and, quality becomes more emphasized and realized. Leaders who do the unexpected for the benefit of others are like a precious gem.

IDEA #48: PASSION FOR LEADERSHIP

Being passionate about being a real leader can reflect a sincere heart for leadership and all it entails. It is not always easy to be a real leader. Challenges have to be faced. Difficulties need to be addressed. Things don't always go as planned. Thus, it can be quite helpful to have a zeal for leadership.

It is refreshing to observe leaders who have a passion (enthusiasm) for leadership. When one is passionate about being a great leader, and acts on the passion by doing what is right, s/he may achieve extraordinary results. Prodigious leaders are *not* people who are merely "placed" in leadership positions (regardless of how the placement occurred). Quite the contrary, they are extraordinary (phenomenal) persons who one might assert were *divinely chosen* or *born* to be great (albeit, real leaders). It is almost as if their life's experiences, positive and/or negative, prepared them to be great leaders. Their ability to transform themselves, others and situations from negative to positive, for example, demonstrate their passion for doing better and helping others do the same.

Passion for leadership is needed esp. when there is a monumental need for real leaders. Followers will most likely find it easier to follow a leader who has a passion for leadership. One way the passion is evident is in the leader's honest desire to help others. Anybody can be concerned with themselves or a group representative of similar thoughts. It does not take much effort. But, it takes real leaders, with a passion for leadership, to be interested in the betterment of *all* others. To do this takes deliberate, meaningful and constant effort. One might proclaim: A leader with a passion for leadership is leadership at its best.

IDEA #49: VALUES FOCUSED AND PURPOSEFUL THINKING

Without a doubt, leaders are expected to have a certain level of cognitive abilities. Leaders need to be able to think rationally, realistically, reasonably and responsibly. These four (4) R's can help a leader be focused and purposeful in his- or her-thinking.

Rational thinking implies being able to understand or comprehend information, as well as make decisions, in a levelheaded or composed manner. Realistic thinking suggests an awareness of the need for cognition based on what is representative of being possible or probable (even if others consider it "far-fetched"). Reasonable thinking is a means of interpreting content in such a way that it is practical, for instance, to implement. Responsible thinking reflects an attitude of accountability for one's actions. The 4 R's are the basis for focused and purposeful thinking.

Leaders who value focused and purposeful thinking will embrace the importance of intelligent thought. They will want to be: discerning; able to articulate ideas; and, equipped to make the right decisions at the right time. In essence, leaders who adopt the philosophy of "values focused and purposeful thinking" represent those who truly want to think and act with integrity. Their emphasis will be on thought processes and actions that are reflective of honesty, truthfulness and proven factual. Clearly, there should be an onus for all leaders to embrace this philosophy.

As a springboard to the importance of cognitive abilities, leadership should demonstrate an inner self-awareness to further cultivate their strengths, manage weaknesses, improve chances for opportunities of positive results and change threats (i.e., pressures) into constructive criticism. The aforementioned will be helpful to a leader towards developing and sustaining the philosophy of "values focused and purposeful thinking".

IDEA #50: LOGICAL AND ANALYTICAL

Real leadership requires being able to think logically and analytically. Leaders are regularly confronted with the need to make important decisions. In some cases, decisions need to be made on-the-spot. At other times, there is a certain timeframe involved when the decision is warranted. For these reasons, leaders need to be ready to make decisions using logic and analysis.

Using common-sense should not be minimized or dismissed due to the sentiment of "who wouldn't use common-sense". Rather, common-sense should be applied to thinking and decision-making on a consistent basis. Leadership necessitates sound thinking. That is, thinking that is logical. When leaders incorporate logic into their thinking they are more likely to have sound reasoning to make better and more informed decisions.

Logical thinking should also include analytical thinking. Leaders should analyze situations and possible outcomes to come up with the most effective decisions. As such, a leader might consider developing a systematic approach to decision-making. For example, the approach may be identifying specific steps to get to a particular desired outcome. Depending upon the situation, in some cases the systematic approach may be rather simple (e.g., the step to take to get from Point A to Point B). However, in other cases, it may need to be more detailed. For instance, identifying and mapping out determinants and specific functions to consider for developing a highly qualified team of professionals.

When logic and analysis are discussed, two additional points are relevant: asking questions and critical thought. Leaders need to be very comfortable with asking questions. Moreover, they should typically have a series of relevant questions to pose for any given topic. The idea is to gather as much information as possible. Informed decisions are, in part, based on information derived from asking the right questions. Formulating and asking questions encourages critical thought.

When leaders apply critical thought as part of the decision-making process, it increases the likelihood of making the right decision versus a haphazard one. Critical thought includes an awareness of varying possibilities with the goal of choosing the one that is most appropriate, best likely to result in a positive outcome and clearly reveals integrity. It should be apparent to others who value integrity that the decision made was, indeed, a *wise decision*. Leaders, therefore, should model logical and analytical thought.

IDEA #51: CAN TELL A STORY TO GET OTHERS TO THINK

Leaders who are able to convey thoughts and ideas in unique ways may be able to communicate more effectively with others. Although as human-beings we have many similarities, there are also distinctions about each person making him or her unique. Leaders who understand the similarities and differences can find creative ways to communicate to be able to reach everyone. One method leaders might consider is communicating with stories.

Articulating ideas by means of a story can help the listeners gain a better understanding of what is being conveyed. Also, they may be more interested in what is communicated. When followers are attentive to the message delivered, they are more apt to higher levels of comprehension. This can lead to a better likelihood of ensuring what is expected is actually accomplished. Leadership clearly encompasses effective communication. Telling a story to express an idea may be effective.

Some leaders may find is easy to use this method of communication. Others, however, may deem it more challenging. To begin incorporating the use of telling a story, a leader may opt to begin with including analogies, for example. Explanations which include expressions of similarities help the listener to use comparisons as a means of better understanding. The same can be said of correlating information to other information or finding linkages to ideas. Interestingly, more ideas are likely to emerge when the audience is able to relate ideas to something else.

Relational thinking, in a sense, can be based on the telling of a story. Different scenarios, and time periods, for instance, but the same concept can yield thoughts and ideas previously undiscovered. Suppose the leader is interested in improving the operations of a specific unit with the goal of increasing quality and productivity. The leader may gather those in the unit and tell a story by presenting two operational situations. In telling the story, it may include references to relevant current or historical events. In turn, the references to outside events may spark ideas in the minds of the listeners. Thereby, the leader sets the foundation for thoughts and ideas which may result in innovative ways to improve the unit's operations.

IDEA #52: KNOWS HOW TO REASON WITH OTHERS

Leadership necessitates the capability of reasoning with others. Humans are not without limitations. As such, leaders do not have limitless authority. They are not omnipotent. Rather, they are individuals who should appreciate having opportunities to reason with others as well as positively influence and motivate others. True leaders want to be able to convince others of the value of doing what is right.

Influencing others in the right way is both impressive and commendable. It takes insightful leaders to do this. Leadership entails being knowledgeable. That is, leaders need to "know". They need to be able to recognize the importance of what others dismiss. This requires being discerning. Leaders should certainly consider the suggestions of others (esp., those with expertise in specific areas) by way of reasoning with them. However, they should be able to identify the best solution for a given situation. Being results-oriented, true leadership suggests being able to distinguish between right and wrong.

When a leader reasons with others, a distinguishing factor should be in the leader's desire to motivate them in a positive manner. Leaders who embrace and reflect optimism tend to be easier to reason with as a means towards improvement. One mechanism for reasoning is use of a cause and effect strategy. Discussions inclusive of this strategy typically encourage reasoning since the communication will entail some level of intuitiveness. The leader who is able to demonstrate being perceptive can reason with others and motivate them towards positivity.

Leadership includes being cognizant of factors that can make it difficult to reason with some people. There are some people who are simply unwilling to consider positive possibilities. Others are not interested in being optimistic about their organization. Thus, leaders need to find effective means for curtailing negative attitudes. Ironically, reasoning with difficult people can end up being enlightening for the leader. Situations like these help the leader to grow intellectually and stimulates more thought as the leader considers additional ways to reason with the disenchanted, for instance. In time, it is hopeful either the leader or someone the leader designates, if applicable and appropriate, will be able to reason so soundly that the person becomes positively influenced and motivated to completely and confidently buy-in to what the leader is communicating.

IDEA #53: EXERCISES PATIENCE

Patience is, perhaps, one of the most challenging character traits to develop. As a leader, having patience can be really helpful. When patience is nurtured, there is no overwhelming desire for a quick, fast or rapid response to arbitrary matters. Moreover, being patient allows for better thinking and decision-making. Leadership should comprise being patient. Without a doubt, leaders will be put in positions where they will have to *wait*. Therefore, knowing how to exercise patience is advantageous.

Today, society seems to embrace whatever is "fast". People want things done quickly. Rapid response appears to be more desirous each passing day. Of course, there are certainly situations where a quick response is needed (e.g., when it is a matter of immediate health, safety and well-being). But, every situation does not require responding quickly. In some cases, it is actually better to wait awhile. Have you ever made a decision relatively fast only to later have preferred to wait and allow some time to make a better decision? Leaders need to know how to determine when to act quickly and when to be patient and wait.

When making organizational changes, for instance, ideally there will be some type of process involved. This suggests there will be a timeframe needed prior to complete implementation of the change. To rush and make changes may hamper the change effort. For example, there may be negative receptivity about the change. Issues may be overlooked, or not addressed, resulting in changes that make things worse. Leadership with an awareness of the importance of patience will ensure each step of the process is taken to ensure minimal problems (preferably none) occur when the change is implemented. Patience can be a truly valuable character trait for a leader.

IDEA #54: BE FLEXIBLE

When a leader is flexible, it makes it so much easier to deal with the unknown (for the leader and others). A flexible leader can easily start, stop, change direction, etc. There is no ardent need for inflexibility in some situations. Stress will likely be minimized when leadership is flexible, too. Being flexible allows the leader to be more relaxed and willing to consider other options. An unnecessarily rigid leader might negatively affect the organization by having demands that are too strict or impossible to meet within an allotted time. Fundamentally, there are likely numerous occasions when leadership flexibility can sort of "calm" the atmosphere. People will likely thrive when there is an appropriate level of leadership flexibility observed.

Of course, depending on the situation, there are times when a leader needs to be stern. This is typically when the situation is of extreme importance. In these cases, flexibility may not be acceptable due to the need for actions to be carried out in a specific manner. At such times, communicating the importance of completing tasks in a precise way will help others understand why flexibility is not appropriate. For this reason, leaders need to know when they can be flexible and when they can't. Understanding circumstances where flexibility is acceptable is just as important as understanding the conditions under which being flexible is inappropriate.

In most organizations, for certain tasks there is a need for standards and/or rules (e.g., to promote uniformity) whereby flexibility is not applied. However, there are also guidelines allowing some degree of flexibility. While standards may be resolute, for example, guidelines may be a way to give advice or serve as a recommendation. Both can be observed in most organizations and effective leaders make sure there is regular communication about each type, based on the organization. Leadership encourages employee empowerment, esp. predicated on established guidelines, by being flexible and allowing employee input when possible.

IDEA #55: HAVE KNOWLEDGE OF OPERATIONS MANAGEMENT

Leaders who know how various areas of the organization functions are better equipped to make informed decisions about the organization. Operations management knowledge helps leaders clearly define areas where changes may be necessary as well as propose appropriate solutions to existing operational problems. The leader does not necessarily have to be an expert in operations management. But, having some understanding is useful.

The operations of an organization are varied and depend on the needs of each department, for example. Of course, leaders must know who is responsible for managing different sectors of the organization. This is rather simple, yet important. Communications with departmental managers, for instance, allows leaders to be more comfortable with the suggestions they propose. The managers benefit, too, since they will be more likely to communicate the need for possible changes within their particular area. Leaders also will require some level of understanding of each area of the organization.

How each department operates, and is managed, is fundamental to the leader's capacity to make the right organizational decisions. From an operations management viewpoint, leaders may find there is a need for proficient competence in regards to, for example: departmental strategies; internal and external customer relations; costs factors relative to functioning; matters related to quantity and quality; any specialized processes; supply and demand particulars; logistics considerations; and, workforce complexities. As such, a leader's level of comprehension of operations management can serve as a catalyst to making impactful decisions for the overall organization.

IDEA #56: ORGANIZED INTELLECTUALLY

Real and genuine leaders, arguably, have the ability to think in ways beyond the average thinker. Their thinking is not necessarily based on having a high IQ (intelligence quotient). Rather, it is based on a keen ability to be organized intellectually. A principle to being organized intellectually might begin with an interest in intellectual pursuits. Leadership involves, to a large degree, wanting to *know* and then actually *knowing* some things.

When a leader is organized intellectually, rational thinking is apparent. The leader does not base everything, esp. important matters, on solely feelings or wishful thinking. Quite the contrary, the leader will purposely take the time to create relevant scenarios to diagnose the underlying problem, study the key issues, reflect on possible solutions and alternatives, and use logic to justify resolutions. Is there room for theoretical considerations when a leader is organized intellectually? Yes, if the theory or hypothesis is sensible, can be explored or researched and can be applied, if it makes sense to do so.

As human-beings, of course, leaders will invariably incorporate some degree of feelings in their thought processes. However, as much as possible, feelings should not be the sole basis for thinking. Feelings may or may not be justified. Feelings can be interpreted incorrectly. Moreover, feelings (and wishful thinking) alone may outright lead to fanciful decisions with no merit. Therefore, leaders need to equip themselves with thorough information based on indisputable facts. Then, the aforementioned can be used to determine emphatically the best decision. The value of being organized intellectually is realized when a leader is *sincerely* interested in being duly informed and takes distinct measures to ensure making the right decisions.

IDEA #57: APPRECIATES STRESS MANAGEMENT ACTIVITIES

Typically, in the workplace (and in life in general) people will use or associate with the term "stress". However, unfortunately, many fail to identify, use and appreciate stress management techniques. Leaders, in particular, should consider incorporating stress management activities into their lives. The benefits of doing so may positively impact the leader personally and professionally.

The types of stress management techniques or activities can vary. It truly depends on the individual to determine what works best for him or her. For some people, reading a novel or book relieves stress. Walking and exercising are physical activities that one may incorporate to help reduce stress. Of course, it is important to consult one's physician prior to engaging in exercise activities. Communicating with others, perhaps, is a way to overcome stress. Taking a moment to engage in positive conversations with others can help one to focus on something more optimistic while alleviating stress. For some people, watching a movie that has lots of good humor might help to reduce stress. Laughing is a way to feel good in the moment; thus, it will likely have a positive effect on reducing negative stress levels. Still others may find it necessary and beneficial to simply be alone and just relax. Getting adequate rest (sleep) is important, too. Whichever activity(ies) a leader chooses, the key is to actually use it or incorporate it into his or her schedule as needed.

Leadership necessitates being able to "get away", so to speak, for a moment. Continuous engagement in work-related tasks without taking a break can actually make it more difficult for the leader to make the best decisions. Clear and more effective thinking is likely to be realized when negative stress is dealt with on a regular basis. For some leaders, they may add the stress management activity to their daily schedule. Other leaders may deem it preferable to use a stress management activity on an ad hoc (e.g., as needed) basis. The leader makes the determination of what method is best suited for him or her. But, to some degree, stress management activities should be identified and used in the leader's life.

When leadership appreciates stress management activities, it is more likely the organization overall will be encouraged to engage in stress management activities. Leaders will understand the value of such activities as a means to benefit themselves as well as others in the workplace. It is possible, then, stress management activities may become a norm of the organization. Leaders who want the workplace environment to thrive will tend to motivate others therein to find healthy ways to minimize or reduce the negative effects of stress. Workplace activities like team-based games, for example, may be effective as a means to help alleviate a stressful work atmosphere, too. Leaders may find the benefits of appreciating stress management activities can help not only themselves but others in the workplace.

IDEA #58: AVOIDS ARROGANCE, PRIDE & EGOTISM

Arrogance, pride and egotism...pick one...they all can end in a leader's ultimate failure. Leaders who desire long-term effectiveness and success should refrain from being arrogant, prideful or egocentric. To some leaders, it may appear that such actions are beneficial immediately or in the short-term. However, eventually, it is likely these actions will result in the leader having a failed leadership term or tenure. Ironically, most people will, to some degree, have to deal with their own tendency to be arrogant, prideful or egotistical. Therefore, those in a leadership position should pay close attention to their own thoughts and behaviors in an effort to avoid arrogance, pride and egotism.

Self-centeredness might just be the one distinct way a leader mistakenly allows one of the three elements (arrogance, pride or egotism) to foster and dominate his or her behavior and actions. Too much focus on self, one's own desires, an overindulgence in selfish whims and/or an overwhelming pursuit of what will satisfy one's own desire can lead to an imbalance of thoughts. Balanced thinking or cognition includes thoughts, leading to behaviors, which represent considerations of others, too. The idea, itself, of *leadership*, is to have a *sincere* aspiration for the well-being of others.

When a leader has a sincere goal or objective that benefits others (and not merely him or her solely), the leader is more likely to make the right decisions. It should be mentioned, too, that the leader's decisions and actions should not be only for the benefit of those in agreement with him or her. Rather, regardless of the viewpoints of others, a *genuine* leader will seek what is best, right and respectable (decent) for *all* involved. Leaders of this caliber can make positive transformations that epitomize and embody the true essence of leadership: To make the lives of others better. The aforementioned statement expresses the sentiment underlying the premise that, unfortunately, all leaders are not genuine, real, true leaders (since every person in a leadership position is not interested in bettering the lives of those they are leading—perhaps due to arrogance, pride and egotism).

Leadership is a tremendous responsibility. It should not be taken lightly. Leaders, therefore, should embrace meekness, humility and selflessness (and avoid arrogance, pride and egotism). These are the character traits of leaders who will likely have historically long-term, lasting and positive illustrations of leadership effectiveness.

IDEA #59: THE RIGHT ATTITUDE

Why is a leader's attitude important? Attitude showcases one's outlook. A *positive* attitude will likely promote a positive atmosphere. An *optimistic* attitude can encourage others to have a favorable perspective. An attitude representative of *realism* may spark discussions that are practical (i.e., useful and expedient) and do not waste time. A leader with an attitude that fosters *innovation* will likely be ambitious towards future possibilities. The right attitude can reflect one, a combination of, or all of the aforementioned.

Being around a leader with a positive attitude may, by some followers, be considered remarkable. Leaders who are uplifting tend to encourage others to be likewise. Organizations would do well to have leaders who are inspiring and know how to work in ways to enable others to be inspiring. Positivity can be an effective means towards organizational improvement. A positive mindset can help one see beyond the challenges. The challenges, then, become opportunities. The opportunities reveal possibilities before untapped. Thus, a positive attitude can result in a leader making distinct and extraordinarily great decisions beyond what anyone could have thought possible.

Optimism encourages hopefulness that is properly placed. Leadership has an element of hopefulness that is best represented when the hope is based on rational and well-reasoned expectations. Leaders have to make decisions regularly. Therefore, it is helpful to have an optimistic demeanor prior to decision-making. The people observing the leader's optimism will probably have more confidence in the leader and his or her abilities. Moreover, when a leader is optimistic, there is a tendency to have confidence that is rooted in reality.

Leadership needs to encompass the ability to be astute when it comes to timeliness. This implies a leader being able to ascertain what is permissible and what is not when it comes to effective communications. Discussions are necessary; however, the right discussions are best and warranted. Discussions that do not advance the leader's ability to be well-informed and yield in making appropriate decisions can be time-wasters. In essence, leaders should be interested in discussions that are realistic in nature. Leadership should emphasize the necessity for communications that are useful and expedient.

Leaders with an attitude that focuses on innovation can be instrumental in sustaining an organization as well as moving the organization forward. Innovation is a term that is rather common today. It is widely used. Yet, in some ways, perhaps, it is misunderstood. Innovation can be a slight change or a drastic change. The idea is, simply put, to make something better by improving it. Based on this understanding, leaders can make it a point to have an innovative mentality whereby possibilities are continuously considered.

The right attitude is a key component for effective leadership. The leader is at the forefront of the organization. Having the right attitude can help the leader realize potentials beyond the norm. The organization may reach uncharted heights due to having a leader who possesses the right attitude.

IDEA #60: DELEGATE, DELEGATE, DELEGATE

Leadership typically requires a multitude of tasks to complete. It is inconceivable for one person to "do it all". Leaders, therefore, need to be able to delegate certain tasks and responsibilities to others. For some in leadership positions, this may not be as easy as it seems. Leaders need to be able to *trust* the person to whom important tasks will be delegated to. That is, the leader wants to trust the person will successfully accomplish the task (i.e., do so correctly) as well as complete the task on time. Additionally, the leader needs to trust the person will be accountable and responsible for his or her actions relative to the designated task.

One of the essential abilities of leadership is delegation skills. Interestingly, other skills seem to get more attention than delegation. Yet, if a leader does not embrace the need to delegate he or she will likely either perform in a substandard manner or completely fail miserably. Some tasks are necessary and/or required; but, they can be accomplished by someone other than the leader. The leader may need to, for instance, follow-up and ensure the task was completed. But, the leader does not have to actually be the person to do the task. Therefore, leaders should determine which tasks can be delegated to others and which tasks need to be completed specifically by the leader.

Acknowledging the need to delegate is only as good as having the right people to delegate to. The leader's trust level should be high in that the leader is confident the person delegated to complete certain tasks can be counted on to do so accurately and in a timely manner. This infers the person must have the talent, skills and abilities necessary to do the work. When a leader is aware that these character traits exists, it is likely easier to have confidence in the abilities of others to do the tasks competently.

The person needs to have the right attitude or mindset such that he or she sincerely wants to help the leader and be considered as an asset (valuable person) by the leader. Delegating to persons who are responsible and accountable for their actions is very helpful towards making leaders comfortable with making decisions to delegate. When a leader has confidence in, and trusts, the persons that he or she delegates work to, the leader will have more time and energy to do even more for the benefit of the organization and its stakeholders. When possible, delegate!

IDEA #61: IN SERVICE FOR OTHERS MINDSET

Leaders with a *service* mindset are fascinating. You might find them helping others in ways most would not. For example, this type of leader will work alongside followers to help accomplish the mission. Leaders of this caliber, for instance, will "get their hands dirty" so to speak. Typically, they do not consider themselves in a lofty (superior) manner. Rather, they are mindful of the impeccable benefits of working with, as well as serving, others. Some of the most important benefits of being in service for others may be more so spiritual. Thus, it is perhaps inherent for this type of leader to be considered humble by others.

Helping others is really a key part of effective leadership. Leaders have a responsibility to make things better. More importantly, they have a responsibility to make a positive impact (by way of decision-making, for example) on others. This is a tremendous responsibility. It requires contemplation of possible solutions, consideration of options and alternatives, and taking appropriate action. Moreover, there is a necessity for the sincere desire (i.e., will) to make decisions for the betterment of all (versus some) at least to some degree or in some way.

It is reasonable to expect a real leader to demonstrate having an in service for others mindset. Real leaders, serve! How leaders serve may vary. Nonetheless, real leaders will find ways to serve others. When leaders serve, they encourage and motivate others to serve, too. These leaders lead by example in getting others interested in serving as well. An in service to others *norm* is likely to develop, at least to some extent, in the organization. When an organization is led by a leader with a willingness to serve others attitude, the organization may experience positive effects such as improvements in professionalism at all levels of the organization.

Perhaps, it takes *special* leaders (i.e., those with distinct character traits) to embrace and exhibit an in service for others mindset. "Special" in the sense of being "not your average person" in a leadership position.

That is, they do not thrive on titles, accolades, or other means purposely used to reflect high-mindedness. Quite the contrary, they are interested in uplifting others. It may be plausible, then, to suggest leaders with an in service for others mindset are dynamic human-beings, designed and equipped for extraordinary work (service).

IDEA #62: FORGIVING

Everyone makes mistakes. These three words convey a simple, easy to understand, message. Yet, it is amazing how so many people tend to either dismiss this fact or choose to only apply it to others— not themselves. Since "everyone makes mistakes", it is necessary to acknowledge: everyone needs forgiveness. Ironically, these three words "everyone needs forgiveness" most people want to apply to themselves; but, in turn, fail to apply it to others. Mistakes and forgiveness go hand-in-hand. Human-beings make mistakes; therefore, human-beings need forgiveness. Leaders understand this concept and apply it to themselves and others.

Leaders, as human-beings, will undoubtedly make mistakes. Hopefully, the mistakes will be minimal and infrequent. Nevertheless, mistakes will happen. Of course, some mistakes can be avoided by getting, for instance, the best information, data and facts that are available on the subject matter. Additionally, refusing to compromise on essential and properly based principles, values and moral convictions helps, too. To deny that one makes mistakes is not realistic. It is a fantasy. It is unreal. A common-sense approach is to acknowledge one's ability to make decisions and choices based on sound research (from proven reliable sources), rational thinking, logical considerations, proficient analysis and critical thought. Doing so will help one to make better, more informed, decisions and choices. However, common-sense dictates that even when the aforementioned is done, sometimes mistakes in decision-making will still occur. Why? One reason is because of human error. Humans are not perfect. Therefore, information from humans may include errors. If the errors are minimal, it is likely any mistake in decision-making will be minimal. Conversely, if the errors are major, the mistake in decision-making may be significant. Hence, the need to acknowledge the mistake, sincerely apologize, discard the faulty information, access additional information and resources, and make corrections. Forgiveness will likely follow.

Leaders, can and will, make mistakes. But, followers will do so as well. In some cases, followers may have limited information. At other times, followers may lack sufficient understanding. Still, in other situations, followers may not have the expertise necessary to competently complete tasks. Regardless, there are occasions where the leader will need to forgive the follower. The easiest way for the forgiveness to occur is for the follower to acknowledge the mistake, sincerely apologize, seek direction and make corrections. Forgiveness will likely follow.

IDEA #63: DOES NOT SEEK TO DIVIDE (PROMOTES UNITY)

One prominent character trait of a true leader is this attribute: The leader is a unifier. The leader comprehends the notion that unity builds and division destroys. Remarkably, unity, in its proper context, fosters enthusiasm while acknowledging and embracing individual ideas, talents, skills and abilities. Dividing, on the other hand, admonishes individual thought, creates chaos and relinquishes freedoms. Leaders should encourage an atmosphere where people can thrive, and the organization can thrive. That is, leadership should promote an environment where people respect themselves (i.e., have dignity), respect one another and work together.

People may look different, act different and think different. But, they need to comprehend one important fact: We all are human-beings. This is the one fact that demonstrates how we are *alike*. It emphatically shows the premiere aspect of our being that we have in common. Differences exist as we are wonderfully and uniquely created. Yet, the differences do not outweigh in importance what we have in common (our humanness). While we should appreciate our uniqueness, we should also value our commonality of being human-beings. As such, the focus should be on what unites us versus on what causes division.

True leadership embraces unity. A real leader will want to bring people together as much as possible. This does not mean that the leader is accepting of poor behavior, inappropriate communications, deceitful activities or mean-spirited actions. Leaders know that some people will have the right intentions while, sadly, others will have the wrong intentions. Effective leadership can be instrumental in the transformation process of changing someone with the wrong intentions to someone with the right intentions. Of course, the person has to want to make a positive change in the right direction or be desirous of the truth. Both can be conduits to a willingness to improve (i.e., be transformed). The leader, obviously, needs to have the right intentions foremost to be effective at helping others. The more the organizational atmosphere is filled with people with the right intentions, the better chance for unity.

A true leader, then, does not seek to divide. Unification is the mechanism for effective leadership. People tend to prefer to get along with others. They purposefully want to be in an environment where they can give respect and receive respect. It is reciprocal. A properly unified atmosphere allows for such reciprocity. The leader who seeks to unify, in its proper context, is one who builds, transforms and enlivens others and the organization.

IDEA #64: TOUCHES THE HEARTS OF FOLLOWERS

It takes a special leader to be able to capture (touch) the hearts of followers such that they desire to do their best. Followers need to trust the leader and the vision of the leader. An understanding of what is needed to turn the vision into a reality is expected. But, perhaps even more important is an awareness and comprehension of the followers' purpose and part in the vision being realized. In addition, leadership requires the accomplishment of a mission, certain goals and objectives. Strategic initiatives are developed by leaders to get to the heart of a problem, make organizational enhancements, etc. However, it is the followers who make a significant impact on carrying out the strategy. Thus, they need to be empowered to make certain decisions. Such empowerment can result in the followers having a commitment to the leader in terms of ensuring the strategic initiatives are accomplished. Hence, the hearts of the followers, when touched by the leader, makes them desirous of exhibiting high performance.

Capturing the hearts of followers can make them driven and centered on what the leader needs and expects to be accomplished. Followers who are motivated and focused on the tasks needed to get done will be more likely to do so when they clearly understand their role in the process. When they perceive they are valuable to the completion of a project, or the accomplishment of a task, the tendency is to work at an elevated level.

Followers who purposely have work performance reflective of high productivity levels, high standards and exceptional excellence will likely have been previously empowered to make certain decisions. Empowerment can lead to improved levels of trust between leaders and followers in the organization. Leaders allocate increasing levels of decision-making to followers. Followers reciprocate by having more trust in the leader. Followers increased levels of trust, coupled with performance improvements, is one way to show the effectiveness of the leader's ability to capture the hearts of followers. Once the hearts of followers are touched, the leader needs to ensure this is maintained.

IDEA #65: RELENTLESS DRIVE TO PERSEVERE FOR GOOD

One of the most striking traits of an effective leader is the persistent push to endure for the sake of something *good*. In this context, "good" is referring to righteous or virtuous. Thus, it is not meant for self-serving acts. Leaders of this type understand setbacks may occur or timelines may need to be extended. An awareness of the possible need for adjustments, in some cases, is acknowledged. The leader, however, continues to make advances, to move forward, and to maintain a mindset of "it will be accomplished".

Remarkably, leaders who exhibit the "relentless drive to persevere for good" are often not necessarily recognized as such by some people (e.g., people who are merely interested in self—i.e., benefits to oneself). However, those individuals who are capable of recognizing these kinds of leaders, will most likely be positively impacted in distinct ways. They may look for opportunities to help the leader on his or her journey. Or, they may opt for the chance to "be there" for the leader consistently or at certain specific times. This is important since leaders with this character trait can undoubtedly benefit from the support of others. However, even without the support of others, this type of leader will still persevere. The reason rests with the leader's understanding that it is important to finish the mission, or accomplish the goal, for the betterment of others. Leaders who are determined to do *good* for the benefit of others are truly extraordinary.

History has a profound way of showcasing these effective leaders. In time, their clear acts of doing good for others will come to light. This is certainly not this type of leader's reason for persevering for the sake of good. However, it is a worthy acknowledgement bestowed upon a leader who purposely considers doing what is best for others. Perhaps, in more ways than one, this particular kind of leader is an example of a model leader.

IDEA #66: 3H FOCUS: HOPE, HELP, HONOR

A leader is defined by his or her character and actions. Of course, real leaders have integrity, for instance. Moreover, real leaders are able to inspire confidence, give support or assistance, as well as recognize the achievements of others.

Leaders with honorable character will be examples others with the same persona (or with a willingness to have the same type of persona) will want to imitate. Honorable character is exhibited by a leader having integrity. A leader with integrity is more likely to have a 3H Focus: Hope, Help, Honor.

Encouraging employees to be hopeful, for example, can be instrumental in motivating them to believe in the possibilities of organizational improvements in the future. Aptly placed hope, combined with help, can really make a difference for employees. Help can take on many forms. However, in many cases, in the workplace it is predominately demonstrated by ensuring the right tools are available to complete assigned tasks. Employees are better positioned to be successful, in terms of their workplace responsibilities, when the proper apparatus or mechanism is in place. When employees succeed, especially if the task was difficult, they should be duly recognized. Effective leadership will ensure the accomplishment is celebrated or some type of honor or esteem is given.

A 3H Focus represents a leader's comprehension of the importance and value of employees. Employees should be viewed as assets to the organization. They are the very ones who work diligently for the organization day in and day out. Their contributions can be notable for the organization. Moreover, employees who are appreciated by leadership will likely be instrumental in helping the organization thrive. A leader with integrity and has a 3H Focus is more likely to be cognizant of the aforementioned.

IDEA #67: BELIEVES IN THE VALUE OF EFFECTIVE LEADERS

Perhaps it is fair to say, leaders who consult with other leaders tend to believe in the value of effective leaders. Any person can be "put" in a leadership position. Merely being given or assigned a title, or placed in a position of leadership, does not equate to truly being an effective leader. Leaders who are effective leaders (in the context herein) will have made positive impressions, for instance, on those they have led. To be able to make positive impressions on others, the leader has to value people and seek ways to make improvements that benefit others. Included in the value of people (e.g., followers) is the value of effective leaders. That is, the leader should believe in the value of *other* effective leaders, too. Two ways to demonstrate this value are: a willingness to *study* about and *learn* from effective leaders; and, *consulting* with other effective leaders.

The study of leadership is typically comprised of learning about individuals in various leadership positions from, for example: education, military, private sector (businesses, organizations, corporations), public sector (local, state, federal government), and religious entities. They can be current leaders as well as leaders from the past. Leadership theories may be used to decipher the leader's style. Moreover, analyses of the leaders' effectiveness might also be explored. For someone interested in becoming an effective leader, however, consideration should be given to actually studying and learning from *effective leaders*. To learn is to take the time to truly investigate and comprehend the leader's character, morals, values, principles, motivation or motives for key decisions, performance and outcomes, and positive effects on others. Doing so will be instrumental in assessing whether the leader was really an effective leader (and, perhaps more importantly, a *real* leader).

Consultation with other leaders deemed as effective leaders can be quite helpful to a *new leader*; as well as, *current leaders* striving to become effective leaders. For some, they may have an opportunity to have the effective leader as a mentor. Others may be able to spend a miniscule amount of time with the effective leader. Still others, however, may find they are allowed considerable time to consult with the effective leader (e.g., for research purposes). Regardless of the time allocated, the objective should be to learn as much as possible about the effective leader. To be an effective leader, one must believe in the value of effective leaders.

IDEA #68: COMMITTED TO LEADERSHIP EXCELLENCE

Leadership excellence is reflective of the purposeful act of a leader towards carrying out responsibilities at a high level (i.e., substantially above average). The reliability of the leader is evident based on leadership excellence, too. The leader can be counted on by others to do what is right. When a leader is committed to leadership excellence, it can make a tremendous impact on the leader, followers and all stakeholders. The organization overall, then, can benefit from a leader committed to leadership excellence. It should be mentioned, leadership excellence is not synonymous with high performance or perfection.

Being committed to a high standard of excellence is not exactly the same as high performance. The typical definition of a high-performing leader is one who gets the job done, so to speak. Or, put another way, it could be defined as one who reaches a certain established goal (number, percentage, dollar amount, etc.). Without a doubt, it is very important for a leader to be high-performing in this sense. But, it is also important for a leader to be able to demonstrate high levels of excellence in terms of ethical behavior, meeting (albeit exceeding) any requirements or standards, and displaying integrity at all times. These essential responsibilities associated with being a leader are ultimately more important than the focus on the goal (or number) solely. Moreover, it is the carrying out of these important responsibilities which essentially determine if the leader is reliable as a leader.

A leader who is only focused on achieving a certain goal, without any ethics, integrity and deliberate assurance requirements and standards are met or exceeded, will likely only have "success" for a time (even if it is years). Moreover, at a certain point, all of the leader's "number" accomplishments (or any other accomplishments) will be meaningless and perhaps even forgotten over time, if the leader is not one reflective of integrity, ethical behavior and adhering to standards or requirements.

The leader should be committed to leadership excellence as well as a high-performer.

Leadership excellence does not mean leadership perfection. While a leader should certainly strive for perfection, the leader is well aware that no human-being is 100% perfect, 100% of the time. Yet, striving for perfection helps towards getting as close to perfection as possible. The leader who is committed to leadership excellence will most likely be interested in getting as close as possible to leadership perfection (esp., when it comes to ethics, integrity and ensuring requirements are met or exceeded).

IDEA #69: CONFRONTS WEAKNESSES WITH APPROPRIATE AND PURPOSEFUL ACTIONS

Every human-being has weaknesses. No one is exempt. The key, however, is acknowledging one's weakness and taking deliberate action to address the weakness. For example, if a person has challenges with writing or grammar, it would be a good idea to use the spelling and grammar check feature to minimize errors before sending an email or while preparing an important document. The same applies to leaders. Leaders should be aware of their strengths. However, they should also be honest with themselves about their weaknesses or limitations. This is applicable to the organization and employees as well.

So, what is your weakness(es)? The first step, and perhaps the most difficult, is acknowledgement. Although it may not be one's preference to think about weaknesses, doing so may be liberating. Once the acknowledgement has occurred, the leader can begin to seek ways to address the weakness so that it does not present unnecessary problems. Leaders who truly desire to be and do their best will confront weaknesses (and limitations) with appropriate actions that minimize or resolve the weakness. Moreover, they will apply this concept to the organization, overall, and the employees.

Leadership requires understanding the organization's weaknesses or limitations. Every organization has its challenges—admittedly or not. Effective leaders are well aware of the need for organizational assessments. Determining areas of improvement, for instance, is one way to bring organizational weaknesses to the forefront. Then, the leader can devise strategies to confront the weaknesses. When these strategies are communicated throughout the organization, positive changes can begin to emerge as the strategies are implemented.

An awareness of the weaknesses of employees can be helpful, too. It is not enough for the leader to acknowledge his or her own weaknesses and the organizational weaknesses. All employees have weaknesses as well. Therefore, open communication with employees at all levels can help with encouraging individual, honest, self-analysis to take place. When employees identify their own weaknesses, and the organization provides tools to help the employees, the weaknesses have a lesser chance of being deterrents to the organization's operational effectiveness. Tools can include, for example, resources or trainings. Employees will tend to be more productive, efficient and motivated when their weaknesses are addressed.

For some leaders, this might be a touchy or unwelcomed topic for discussion. From a human nature standpoint, it is quite understandable why this might be the case. Acknowledging one's weaknesses, the organization's weaknesses as well as employees' weaknesses is not easy for every leader to do. Some people, unfortunately, view weaknesses as being somewhat of a failure. But, for an effective leader, it really is wise to acknowledge weaknesses and take appropriate and purposeful actions to minimize or resolve the weaknesses.

IDEA #70: PRAYS, PRAYS AGAIN, AND KEEPS ON PRAYING

The leader who is a believer of Jesus Christ as Lord and Savior should understand the need for, and importance of, daily prayers to Almighty God (see Luke 18:1). For this leader, continuous prayer is a means of remaining in constant communication with the Lord. Thus, constant prayer will likely be the norm for this leader. Prayers, for instance, may begin with the leader's reverence for God. Next, help for others or prayers about others may be reflected. Then, the leader may take some time to pray for areas reflective of his or her personal circumstances and professional endeavors. Although the prayers will not necessarily be the same each time, the leader embraces the notion of praying, praying again, and continually praying.

Admiration for the Lord includes understanding who He is and accepting what His word says. Worshipping Him during prayer as well as highly esteeming Him are aspects of reverence. In addition, fearing God for who He is, and the fact that He is the ultimate judge, may be part of the leader's showing of respect. In essence, the leader acknowledges that the Lord is above him or her and *above all others*. Moreover, the leader shows appreciation for God allowing him or her to be in a position of leadership. To be clear, the leader is well aware of the fact that there is *only one God* (revealed in three persons—God the father, God the Son (Jesus Christ) and God the Holy Spirit); and, He deserves all the glory. The leader who believes this will likely be mindful of this when praying, praying again, and praying continuously.

Leaders with the aforementioned belief will, undoubtedly, pray for others, too. When the leader's heart has been changed by the Lord, a desire to hope for the best for others will materialize. The leader will most likely pray regularly for others. In most cases, he or she will find ways to help others as well. This can be done in numerous ways, for example: volunteering time; being charitable; taking the time to actively listen; and, being supportive or encouraging. The leader's time spent praying on behalf of others will be important especially when led by God to do so. Therefore, the leader will pray for others, pray again and continue praying.

It is common when praying to pray for oneself. A key factor rests in communicating with God about specific situations, events or circumstances—personal and/or professional. The leader will likely be interested in guidance and wisdom from the Lord. Since only God is all-knowing, He is the Perfect One to go to in prayer about everything. The leader who knows this will pray regularly as he or she seeks the best guidance and direction. Moreover, because the leader comprehends that wisdom only comes from God, communication with the Lord will be essential as the leader desires to be an effective leader. This motivation for effective leadership will likely prompt the leader to pray, pray again and keep on praying.

IDEA #71: KNOWS HOW TO FOLLOW

Rarely, if ever, is a leader *a leader* in all aspects of his or her life. Instead it is more likely a leader will be in one or more follower positions, too. While being in a leadership position in the workplace, the leader may also be a follower in other capacities (e.g., when performing volunteer work for a charitable organization). Leadership requires flexibility; and, inclusive in this is the ability to be a follower as opposed to solely a leader. Knowing when, and how, to follow is just as important as being in a leadership position.

When a leader knows how to follow, he or she will be more understanding of other followers and their needs. This understanding will likely help the leader to be more informed as to what is required to ensure followers are equipped with the tools necessary to accomplish their job-related tasks, for instance. Moreover, the leader will be able to better comprehend the dynamics associated with being a follower. For example, some followers require frequent direction and attention. Conversely, there are followers who work well on their own and virtually no guidance is needed. Then, there are followers who may only need assistance occasionally as well as a moderate amount of attention. Understanding these differences can help a leader better understand followers, in general.

Taking the knowledge and experiences gained as a follower can be instrumental in helping the leader noticeably improve in his or her leadership role. Likewise, the leader will likely be able to make a significant impact in the transformation of his or her followers. When followers have a leader, who is aware of what it means to be a follower, they are apt to respond more favorably towards the leader. From the leader's perspective this can result in, for example, organizational changes that are more easily accepted (i.e., with little to no follower dissent or resistance to the change). Due to the likely ease of communication between the leader and the followers, decisions made by the leader can be carried out more efficiently and effectively. Additionally, the leader is better positioned to be understood and respected. Consequently, a leader who has a keen awareness of the dynamics of followers will likely be more understanding of followers and show better respect for them. Knowing how to follow is beneficial for the leader and those he or she leads.

ABOUT THE AUTHOR

Dr. Pamela Loyd, Ph.D. has been an educator for over 19 years. She has taught undergraduate and graduate students (including students in MBA programs) at colleges and universities. In addition, she has professional experience training corporate employees (e.g., trainings related to Quality Management/Statistical Process Control). As an educator, she has a passion for helping adults learn. In particular, her interests include helping company employees understand the importance of, need for, and ways to apply, exemplary "soft skills" at all levels of the organization: employee, supervisor, management and executive leadership. Dr. Loyd also has professional experience in positions requiring supervision, management and leadership. She is a proponent of helping develop employees, supervisors, managers and leaders. As a side note, yet reflective of her passion, she looks forward to using her poetic skills as a lyricist (songwriter) to write Christian and Gospel lyrics which will hopefully be set to music in the near future.

INDEX

Printed in the United States
By Bookmasters